M000036493

Praise for
ATTEND

"Laura Davis Werezak writes thoughtfully about the difficulties and joys of establishing a spiritual practice amidst the many distractions of contemporary life. She explores her own experience together with reflections on Scripture and the rich literature of Christian spirituality to create a clear-headed, sweet-tempered invitation into simple daily practices that can open us to the everyday wonder of 'God with Us.' I already have a list of people with whom I want to share this lovely book."

—Maxine Hancock, PhD, professor emerita of spiritual theology at Regent College, Vancouver, BC, Canada

"Laura Davis Werezak's examination of simple practices is an invitation to see the entire world differently. Like the current books on mindfulness, *Attend* offers to help us to slow our bodies and hearts and 'practice the presence of the present.' But Werezak wants more than enriched lives: the exercises she suggests point us towards worship. *Attend* is a wise, beautiful, winsome call to sacramental living."

—Kurt Armstrong, Anglican lay minister and author of *Why Love Will Always Be a Poor Investment: Marriage and Consumer Culture*

"*Attend* meets the reader in a safe place but doesn't let us stay there. Laura gradually brings us out of our conformity to our comfort and lets us try new experiences that elevate our view of God and allow us to see ourselves in a better light."

—Kevin Young, national director for Cru High School and author of *Thirty Days to Connect to God's Heart: A Primer*

"*Attend* is a book for the distracted and soul weary. With gentleness and creativity it invites us to stretch our bodies, our hearts, our minds in ways that open us to the world around us—and to the God who has already stretched toward us in Christ."
　　　　—Dr. Cynthia Wallace, assistant professor of English at
　　　　St. Thomas More College, University of Saskatchewan
　　　and author *Of Women Borne: A Literary Ethics of Suffering*

"This is one of the few times someone has put into words the character of a relationship with a personal God that I can understand and into which I feel I could enter. Thank you."
　　　　　　　　　　—Emily Ganzer, minister's wife and
　　　　　　　　　　　　　　mother, Toronto, ON

ATTEND

ATTEND

Forty Soul Stretches Toward God

LAURA DAVIS WEREZAK

Faith
Words

NEW YORK BOSTON NASHVILLE

FaithWords
Hachette Book Group
1290 Avenue of the Americas, New York, NY 10104
faithwords.com
twitter.com/faithwords

First Edition: February 2017

FaithWords is a division of Hachette Book Group, Inc. The FaithWords name and logo are trademarks of Hachette Book Group, Inc.

The publisher is not responsible for websites (or their content) that are not owned by the publisher.

The Hachette Speakers Bureau provides a wide range of authors for speaking events. To find out more, go to www.hachettespeakersbureau.com or call (866) 376-6591.

Library of Congress Cataloging-in-Publication Data has been applied for.

ISBNs: 978-1-4555-4148-5 (hardcover), 978-1-4555-4147-8 (ebook)

Printed in the United States of America

WOR

10 9 8 7 6 5 4 3 2 1

For my grandparents Glenn and Frances Ketchum,
who lived powerful lives of quiet good deeds,

and

for Loren and Mary Ruth Wilkinson,
who, like Tom Bombadil and Goldberry,
teach many the power of attentive, creative hospitality
along a weary road

Contents

PART II. REST

PART III. QUIETNESS

For thus said the Lord G<small>OD</small>, the Holy One of Israel,
"In **returning** and **rest** you shall be saved;
In **quietness** and in **trust** shall be your strength."

Isaiah 30:15 <small>ESV</small>

Learning to Attend to God

Years ago, when I was in my midtwenties and deeply lonely for God, I lost the ability to connect with God. As a young woman growing up in church, I experienced God through Bible reading, prayer, and Sunday worship services, but at some point, those quit working for me. When I opened the Bible, the pages were oddly blank. When I sat down to pray, I asked God for things I wanted, then fell into an awkward silence, unsure what else to say. When I came to worship, the music and words whipped up emotions, but I wondered what—if anything—was beyond the frenzy and the empty feeling in my stomach.

For a few years, much longer than I should have, I doggedly kept trying to come to God in the ways that used to work for me, and each time I tried again, I hoped. Surely the last failure was just a fluke. *This time*, I would meet God in the Scriptures again. *This time*, I would know what to say to God. *This time*, I would feel God's presence at our church. I went back to the same approaches over and over again, but expected different results. I was slow to realize that I could not go back.

In my life with God, I stood at the bottom of a jagged cliff face that went straight up. If the goal was life with God at the top of the mountain, I had come this far along the level trail to the foot of this cliff with only three simple climbing tools—study, prayer, worship. But even if I gathered up all my effort and used up all my strength, these tools were blunt, bent out of shape, and not working anymore.

I longed for the connection with God I felt as a young person, and I was determined to get to the top of that mountain. But there didn't seem to be any way forward. I sat down with my back against the wall, muttering angry words until fear gnawed away my longing and almost convinced me to give up on connecting with God. There in that low place I began to see things from a different perspective. A way forward appeared as I slowed down to give my attention to the quiet, good deeds it takes to sustain life every day. The simplicity of this new approach surprised and puzzled me.

To attend is a physical posture

The word *attend* means literally "to stretch toward." I was startled the first time I read this definition in a book about attention deficit disorder, because I do not think of attention as a physical posture. I think of attention as mental focus—a measure of how long a student can sit still in class and listen to a lecture or how long my eyes linger on an article online—but I do not think much about the body attached to that attention span.

In fact, my husband, Clint, and I often repeat the same conversation. We switch roles, but we end up in the same place again and again.

"What did you say?" I bellow over the noise of water running in the sink and squeals of delight from our two young daughters. Over hum of dishwasher, grind of disposal, lilt of music, babble of television. Over the drama of a movie trailer on my smart phone. Over the quiet moments that I fill with focus.

"Never mind, it's not important," he says.

"No really, what did you say? I want to know." My eyes flick to him and back to my busy hands.

"Well, then, why don't you *pay attention?*"

When I am at my best and I do give Clint my full attention, I stretch my neck slightly in his direction. I tilt my ear toward him. I turn my eyes. My face and my heart beating in my chest are open and vulnerable toward him. He wants this type of focus from me.

But I often fail to give him my full attention. I am distracted by noise and silence, work and leisure, and I may say with my mouth, "I want to know," but my posture gives Clint a different message.

To attend to those I love, I have to use my body. I have to stretch, tilt, and turn.

To attend to God is also a physical posture

We also know God by stretching, by orienting our physical bodies toward God.

Throughout the Christian Scriptures, God asks people over and over again for their attention. But God does not demand that they *pay attention*—as though attention were a physical object they could give, or a debt they could repay. What God asks is:

- Give ear and hear. (Isaiah 28:23)
- Incline your ear. (Isaiah 55:3)
- Listen. (Deuteronomy 4:1)
- Look to God. (Isaiah 51:1)
- Turn your face. (Ezekiel 14:6)
- Do not turn aside. (1 Samuel 12:20–21)
- Do not plug your ears. (Zechariah 7:11)
- Give attention. (Isaiah 28:23)

It is Israel's physical postures of attention and distraction that show us whether or not God's people were in a good relationship with God.

This face-to-face relationship is also what people long for as they ask God over and over:

- Make your face shine on your servant. (Psalm 31:16)
- Look. (Psalm 80:14)
- Hear my cry/Listen. (Psalm 61:1)
- Incline your ear to me. (Psalm 86:1)
- Do not hide your face from me in the day of my distress. (Psalm 102:2)

Both God and humans both seem to long for the same thing, then. We want to know that the other person in this relationship is stretching toward us with the basic postures of attention.

Finding God's puzzling ways in the world

In Isaiah 30:15, God spoke to the people of the nation of Israel through the prophet Isaiah, to call them to face-to-face relationship. Their country was facing attack from the powerful nation of Assyria, and they had to decide where to look for help and support. Isaiah writes:

> *For thus said the Lord GOD, the Holy One of Israel,*
> *"In returning and rest you shall be saved;*
> *In quietness and in trust shall be your strength."*

It was a strange national defense strategy. As I sat at the bottom of the cliff face waiting, it was as if Jesus came to meet me there and handed me this verse. Returning, rest, quietness, and trust sounded good to my soul, like a breath of fresh air, or a new way forward, even if they felt counter to my own methods. I thought about the words for a long time and began to understand grace again. I was not going to make it to God by striving on my own, by pressing forward, trying harder, praying louder, studying longer, or showing up at church every time the doors were open. I knew that. "Getting to the top of the mountain" wasn't even the goal. God wanted me to turn my face, to choose to return to our relationship and find rest, quietness, and trust there. God wanted my full attention. Relationship with God wasn't waiting at the top once I made the grueling climb. Jesus was right there next to me, attentive and waiting, a good Guide. He knew the way up new paths I had never seen before, if I was willing.

It was harder than I expected to look God in the face. In one way, we were old friends: I'd prayed to accept Jesus into my heart at five years old and spent my childhood and teen years totally in love with his gentle goodness. In another way, though, the tough experiences of my twenties—encountering death and pain in ways I didn't expect—filled me with emotions I didn't know how to deal with: hurt, anger, betrayal. When I looked to God, I couldn't picture a face, or if I did, I'm not sure it was a kind one.

God's face turns toward us

When God's face turns toward us in Jesus, it's a face that often surprises us. It does not fit into our tidy conceptions of what we think God should be like. It is strange that God— who is beyond this world—chose to take on a dusty *human* face in the person of Jesus, and strange the type of face God chose: the face of a helpless baby, a poor refugee child, a plain workingman. Jesus looked into the eyes of God's people two thousand years ago. He saw prophets and servants, fishermen and farmers, Jewish synagogue leaders and Roman tax collectors, determined mothers and mentally ill sons, rich young men and old beggars in rags, foreign soldiers and immigrant women. And looking into their faces, Jesus renewed God's invitation into face-to-face relationship.

Jesus's offer did not go over well. Not everyone liked the God they saw in Jesus. Jesus shocked their sensibilities, rattled their expectations, and threatened the economic, social, and religious systems they set up. They expected God to show up as their mighty King, to kick the Roman Empire out of their nation, to make a throne room in the temple with all the pomp and circumstance worthy of the Creator of the Universe. Instead they got a poor carpenter's son from a small rural town.

Jesus started his so-called ministry by going out to the desert to visit his wild cousin John the prophet, washing in a river, and wandering for forty days. Rather than gathering around him the most promising leaders of his time for an uprising against Rome, Jesus gathered a ragtag group of poor, uneducated, crooked, powerless men and women, then went around the country healing the lame, bringing sight to the blind, and telling people they were freed from the burden of their sins. All the while, he claimed to be the promised One, the way to God. The God revealed in Jesus seemed like a big disappointment.

After a long look into the human face of God, disappointment stung so much that the rulers of God's people decided that this was *not* the God they wanted after all. And so God suffered and died.

But death could not defeat God's desire for relationship with us. Jesus came back to life. He walked, ate, smiled, laughed, and taught those willing to stretch toward him and listen. He ascended to his throne—not the seat of economic, political, or religious power in the temple in Jerusalem, but a throne of justice at the right hand of God in heaven.

The justice Jesus offers to us is the opportunity to live lives of personal freedom beyond what any human system offers. Freedom to live in face-to-face relationship with God and others without shame. Freedom to transform lives and whole societies. Freedom to live in love, joy, peace, patience, kindness, goodness, gentleness, and self-control in any political, social, or physical circumstances. Freedom to offer this relationship with God to anyone, no matter their race, creed, social status, mental ability, or any other marker of their identity. It was a freedom more radical than ever imagined before.

God's invitation for relationship with every human person through Jesus is the promise this book extends to you. But often Jesus's story still perplexes us. It can become so familiar, we can barely look at it. If we cannot physically look into Jesus's face in the twenty-first century, how do we know God?

We know God now in one another

Since the death, resurrection, and ascension of Jesus Christ, we know God's face in face-to-face relationships with one another. The Creator God formed human beings at the beginning to bear God's Image in this world (Genesis 1:28).

If you look at my daughters, you will learn a little bit about what my husband and I are like. Likewise, look at any human being on earth and you learn a little bit about what the three persons of God are like—Father, Son, and Spirit; Creator, Savior, and Counselor; Friend, Lover, and Living Breath. When we are in right relationship with God, our human bodies are temples of God's Spirit. And together we are the Body of Christ in the world. We who stretch our faces toward Jesus with attention reflect the bright Image of God to others.

This is the twofold miracle of Christianity: Any of us can

turn our faces to God, at any time and in any condition, and find transformation. And any of us, over time, can become more like Jesus by looking to him daily.

This process is not perfect. Even in face-to-face relationships, it is often difficult to communicate, to understand, to really know or love another person. Misunderstandings build, and hurt can make it nearly impossible to really see one another. This happens in all types of relationships, in families, with friends, at work.

And yet we can choose to stretch toward one another. We give small gifts of attention. We show up on the doorstep of life, ask, seek, knock, and hope that slowly, one small interaction at a time, we can come to know and trust one another.

I have come through periods of doubt and darkness where the Image of God was hard to see. When Jesus showed up at the foot of that cliff again, the God I met that day broke down my cherished ideas about who God should be and how faith works. Jesus's way forward through returning, rest, quietness, and trust shocked me, offended me, and then piqued my curiosity. I found myself bumping around discovering God in new places I had never expected to see the Savior of the Universe.

That day I began my own journey into small, daily acts of attention. I slowly adopted the physical postures that turned my body face-to-face with God. I encountered God by stretching toward the created world and Image-stamped people one moment at a time. In the same way that we build trust over time between friends, lovers, and families, God rebuilt my trust.

My new encounter with God began with turning my face

toward the God who was already present to me, stretching my neck toward Jesus. It began when I made my first feeble attempts to actually *attend* to God.

Discover for yourself new approaches to God. Rip down the dividing wall between your "time with God" in prayer, reading, and worship and the rest of your everyday life. Look for God in every moment. Expect God to show up everywhere. *Let your daily actions be your prayer, your reading, and your worship.*

When your soul's muscles ache to stretch toward God, but you can't tell where to even start, make a beginning anywhere in this book, with any activity that seems right. Or start at the beginning of the book and work your way to the end. Read during a season of intentional prayer such as Advent (the four weeks leading up to Christmas) or Lent (the forty days leading up to Easter). Read it through in one sitting to see the whole picture, or pause after every chapter to learn with your hands and feet and gut what your eyes have merely glanced over and your mind has only imagined. The power is found in the *doing*. You might read several chapters in one day and try them all, hungry for more and more, or you might read one chapter, mark your place with whatever ribbon, receipt, or scrap of paper you find at hand, then set the book down and try the same activity every day for a week—reading the whole book slowly over nearly a year, and building daily life habits. Read with others or by yourself. Skip a chapter that seems too hard right now. But no matter how you read, *give yourself grace*.

There is no one right way to stretch toward God. This book is not a spiritual checklist. You will discover many, many other tasks, deeds, games, practices, and actions that connect you with God along the way. Pause regularly along the way to check in with your body and soul and to notice how it feels to make these stretches. Just as you would train in short bursts before you run a long race, or as a friendship builds through working side by side on common interests and sharing jokes and stories before you trust someone to help you in a crisis, build your relationship with God by dedicating just a few moments to these quiet good deeds and build up to longer investments of time and trust. Souls are at least as fragile as bodies. They are also stronger than we imagine, if we stretch them with the sensitivity and respect toward the God who loves us and waits for us.

> *The* Lord *bless you and keep you;*
> *the* Lord *make his face shine on you and be gracious*
>   *to you;*
> *the* Lord *turn his face toward you and give you peace.*
>   Numbers 6:24–26 niv

PART ONE

Returning

For thus said the Lord G<small>OD</small>, the Holy One of Israel,
"In **returning** and rest you shall be saved;
In quietness and in trust shall be your strength."

Isaiah 30:15 <small>ESV</small>

Open a window

Stand up, walk over to the nearest window, and open it.

Do you *have* a window that opens? Or are you in one of the dark, dank places in the universe without them, like huge soulless buildings and basement apartments? If you are in one of those places, I'm sorry. I've spent a lot of time in such places.

I once worked in a school where my assigned classroom had no windows to the outside. That room was a miserable place to spend my days. No light, no fresh air. In the summer, we were hot. In the winter, we were even hotter because the building's thermostat was always set to warm the outer classrooms with drafty windows. When a prankster stuck his hand in the classroom door and switched off the lights, it was terrifying. I couldn't see my hand in front of my face.

If you don't have windows, go where you can enjoy one for a few minutes: a different room, a break room, a stairwell, a car. Open it.

When you open the window, you cannot avoid the day's weather. It will roll in through the open space. Heat. Breeze. Chill. Rain. You may find yourself craving a cup of hot tea or needing to anchor papers and books so they don't blow away. You may need to put on a coat or take off a sweater. The word *window* was originally a metaphor, from the Old English words for "wind's eye." Windows provide the wind an entry and an exit. If you open your window, you will find that you have extended an invitation to a peculiar, unreliable guest. You will have to make peace with what happens.

We are increasingly unwilling to take that risk. According to a recent statistic, North Americans spend up to twenty-three hours a day indoors. We are so carefully sealed off from the weather on a daily basis that it is hard to think up polite conversation about the weather anymore, and if I did, I might get a blank look in response. This type of conversation can feel shallow and trite, but there is a politeness in it seasoned with some humility and wonder. It is important to notice the weather. It is good to take a few seconds a day to feel the sun on your face or the cool of the rain or the blast of the snow. Let yourself be present in the world for a moment.

Opening a window is good for your physical health. In *Home Comforts*, a surprisingly modern book on the art and science of keeping house, writer Cheryl Mendelson includes a whole chapter on keeping a house well ventilated by opening windows and letting in fresh air. Victorian housekeepers were well aware of this need, though it fell out of fashion until recently. Now the scientific evidence suggests we need eight changes of fresh air a day circulating in a home to sweep away the humidity, dust, cleaning chemicals, and other pollutants that build up by daily life. My Norwegian grandmother believed this and slept with her window open a crack every night, even through the dead cold of Wisconsin winters. It didn't seem to hurt—she lived well into her eighties.

Opening a window is good for your spiritual health, too. In his *Confessions*, Saint Augustine compared his soul to a house, praying to God: "The house of my soul is too small for you to enter: make it more spacious by your coming. It lies in ruins: rebuild it. Some things are to be found there which will offend your gaze; I confess this to be so and know it well. But who will clean my house?"

As you stand or sit by your open window, imagine that your soul is a house, big or small, with windows still shut tight. The air inside feels oppressive with heat, cold, fumes, moisture, smells. Your thoughts and emotions pace back and forth trapped in stale hallways and rooms with no outlet. Now, throw open a window to let fresh, outdoor air come in.

One of the most neglected and misunderstood names for God is "Holy Spirit." When we visualize the Holy Spirit, we often think of the old King James Version translation "Holy Ghost," and we think of a person who has died and lost their body wafting around eerily. But this name for God comes from Hebrew and Greek words that could also be translated as "Holy Wind" or "Holy Breath." This name of God is less like a creepy ghost and more like fresh air.

Open the windows of your soul house and let God come rushing in. Feel this Holy Wind on your skin, see it blow around your rooms, smell the rain, the soil, the sea, taste its sweetness or saltiness.

My church community prays an old prayer on Sundays at the beginning of the service:

ALMIGHTY God, unto whom all hearts be open, all desires known, and from whom no secrets are hid: Cleanse the thoughts of our hearts by the inspiration of thy Holy Spirit, that we may perfectly love thee, and worthily magnify thy holy Name; through Christ our Lord. *Amen.**

We call this the "collect for purity." It is an invitation to open the windows of our souls. We cannot hide from God. But if we let in the gentle breeze or even the fierce gust of the Holy Spirit, God can set to the good hard work of airing our soul houses.

We open the windows and invite God's Holy Wind to cleanse the air in our hearts so that we can love more perfectly, give credit where credit is due, and live at peace with God and others. So that the air we breathe can be life-giving rather than poisoned by our fears and negative thoughts. So that it can be clean and fresh.

Open a window. Let God's fresh air transform your soul into a home where love can live.

———

*The General Synod of the Anglican Church of Canada, Book of Common Prayer Canada (Toronto: Anglican Book Centre, 1962), 67.

Make your bed

What is the first thing you do every morning when you get out of bed? Put on slippers? Check e-mail or social media on your phone? Stretch and yawn? Pet your cat? Take your dog for a walk? Rub your eyes and frown at the roommate who woke you with a start by turning on every light in the house and rattling every pot, pan, and dish in the kitchen while singing a happy morning song, or at the child who crept in silently and stared at you in the dark until you woke up startled by two eyes shining just inches from yours?

I'm trying to make a new habit. Every morning when I get up, I want to make my bed. To smooth the sheets I spent a night wrestling. To tuck in the unruly blankets until they lie tight across the mattress. To plump up the pillows. Then to stand back for a second to admire.

I am not quite in the habit yet. As I write these words at a desk in my bedroom, fantasizing about a made bed, I blush to realize that the real bed behind me is not yet made. Better late than never.

It seems like such a small thing, but it's amazing the difference a tidy bed can make. At the University of Texas at Austin Convocation in 2014, U.S. Admiral William H. McRaven explained that when he was training to become a Navy SEAL, his supervising officers would come into his bedroom at the barracks every day to make sure he had made his bed properly. McRaven pointed out three reasons why this simple task was so important. First, he said that one small task accomplished will likely lead to another. Second, taking the time to make the bed reminds you that the little things in life matter. And finally, if you have a terrible day in which nothing goes right, at least you can come home to an inviting bed. As he puts it, "A made bed gives you the encouragement that tomorrow will be better."

Making our beds is a small kindness to ourselves, what poet and spiritual writer Kathleen Norris has called "a meaningful expression of hospitality to oneself, and a humble acknowledgment of our creaturely need to make and remake our daily environments."* It is a reminder of the hours we spend in the vulnerability of sleep each night and of the bodies we live in and care for every day.

Making and remaking our daily environments by tucking in sheets, washing our faces, combing hair, flossing and brushing teeth, and cutting toenails are not the glamorous part of life. While these are the things that make up the bulk of our daily lives, other people don't particularly want to see them on social media. The real significance in whether we tuck, wash, comb, floss, and cut is private, for ourselves, not for a public audience. They are intimate acts of kindness.

But in our busy public world, these private actions often seem frustrating, overwhelming, time consuming, invisible, and ultimately unimportant. Time continually erases the work we put into these things. Every night, you will get back in your bed and mess it up again. You will have to wash your face and comb your hair again in the morning. We strive for an impossible ideal, a life that is never messy, feeling the pressure of constant failure, or we give up entirely and live like slobs. *Just leave the stupid bed*, we say to ourselves, and we still feel we've failed. But these extremes miss the meaning behind self-care.

Pressing past both the temptation to tidy endlessly or leave your bed a mess, we can discover the sin of *acedia*, a term used frequently in the early church but largely forgotten today. Identifying acedia and naming it as a sin expose our self-deception. In her book *Acedia and Me*, Norris says, "At its Greek root, the word acedia means absence of care."* Acedia is a form of inattentiveness, an inability to be present in or take pleasure in the world, a turning of our faces away from God and the gifts our Creator has given us and a turning toward distraction, discontent, and boredom.

The body you live in every day, *that* body is the reality given to you by God. Along with its needs, however small, repetitive, irritating, and all-consuming, your body is God's gift to you. As Søren Kierkegaard puts it, "Repetition is reality, and it is the seriousness of life…repetition is the daily bread which satisfies with benediction."† God's benediction, our Creator's blessing to you, the food of everyday life, is hidden in daily, repeated acts of self-care.

Our lives are not made up of money, power, fame, career, or other great accomplishments, luxuries, or pleasures. Not really. Life is being present to quiet good deeds like making our beds. In a wonderful way, these tasks hold the power to give us new life. They offer us a reminder that we are not God, we do not create the world anew every day, but we need our Creator and Sustainer to do that. When we make our beds, we turn our faces back to God at the start of each new day.

Admiral McRaven says, "If you want to change the world, start off by making your bed." You may not ever become an admiral or change the whole world, but making your bed can definitely change your soul. And that matters.

––––––

*Kathleen Norris, *Acedia and Me* (New York: Riverhead Books, 2008).

†Søren Kierkegaard, *Fear and Trembling and Repetition.* Quoted in Kathleen Norris, *The Quotidian Mysteries* (New York: Paulist Press, 1998), 28.

Plant a seed

I have two favorite stories about seeds. The first is found in a book called *Revelations of Divine Love*, which was written by Julian of Norwich way back in the fourteenth century. As she lay on what she thought would be her death bed, Julian had a vision of God. At first she was sure she had lost her mind; she laughed as she told others the story of her "ravings," but wise counselors told her she needed to take it seriously. In her vision, God showed Julian a seed with the power to transform her view of the world. With spiritual eyes, Julian saw a little thing in the palm of her hand, the size of a hazelnut and round as a tiny ball. She says:

> I looked at it with my mind's eye and thought: 'What can this be?' And the answer came in a general way, like this, 'It is all that is made.' I wondered how it could last, for it seemed to me so small that it might have disintegrated suddenly into nothingness. And I was answered in my understanding: 'It lasts and always will because God loves it; and in the same way everything has its being through the love of God.'*

Have you ever held a hazelnut in your hand? It is one of the smallest and roundest of the tree nuts. Yet that little brown nut bursts with the potential to become a huge tree.

The tiny version of Creation that Julian held in her hand, so small it reminded her of a hazelnut, contrasts so strongly with the continually expanding universe we live in. Yet in God's eyes all that exists is as small as a seed. Our Creator sustains it by love. If a tiny speck within it lasts and grows, it grows by the power of love.

The second story I love is one that Jesus tells. He says:

> "God's Kingdom is like seed thrown on a field by a man who then goes to bed and forgets about it. The seed sprouts and grows—he has no idea how it happens. The earth does it all without his help: first a green stem of grass, then a bud, then the ripened grain. When the grain is fully formed, he reaps—harvest time!" (Mark 4:26–29 MSG)

I like Jesus's story because I'm a terrible gardener. I don't even have to go to sleep at night to forget the seeds I've planted. I plant them in the wrong soil. I keep them in the wrong place with too much sun or not enough warmth. I forget to water them and usually discover my plant crispy and dead a week later. But from time to time, those little plants have grown anyway; they have flourished in spite of me. Jesus connects this physical lesson from nature—that it is not the farmer, but God who gives and sustains life—with our spiritual reality. Spiritual growth doesn't happen because of our striving or our effort, but because of God's love.

As you come to the task of planting a seed, you will need to select a seed. It is not as hard as we think. You can find seeds in packets in the grocery store or the hardware store, but your kitchen pantry or the produce aisle are also full of seeds that we've forgotten are seeds—dried beans, popcorn, mustard grains, barley corns, not to mention all the apples, oranges, lemons, berries, avocadoes, and squashes full of living seeds.

Once you have selected your seed, you will need to find some dirt. Just a small cup of dirt will do. It doesn't need to be special. You can beg it off a friend or neighbor, scoop it from your yard, buy some at the store. If the soil is hard, you will need to break it up. Stones are good for growing roots, so leave those in. Poke a hole in your dirt, put your seed in. Cover it over. Give it a bit of water and leave it in a sunny, warm place.

What both Julian's and Jesus's stories tell us as we plant a seed is that no matter how well we provide the right soil, the right amount of water, the right tender care for our seeds, ultimately God is the one who makes a seed grow. In fact, a seed in perfect conditions, in the perfect soil, with just the right amount of warmth, light and water may fail to grow. I could play classical music for it, sing to it, plant it at the right cycle of the moon, feed it all kinds of vitamins, and any other shenanigans. But I cannot make that seed grow.

It is not so different from the fact that I can strive in my spiritual life, I can insert all the right information, warm my emotions with song and conversation, I can jump at every chance to serve in my local church, and ultimately see that my soul is not growing. Because ultimately life, both the life of our seeds and the life of our souls, is given and sustained by God's love.

All we can do as gardeners and growing souls is learn to be present to God as we plant a seed. Like the tiniest seedling that stretches toward the light or blows in the breeze, or like a little plant that stretches thirsty white roots into the darkness of the soil for nourishment, drinking up the rain, we are present to God in weakness, in fragility, and in hope. We are rooted and grounded in God's love. And finally, after witnessing the miracle of growth and waiting for the right time, we will harvest the fruit of that love—flowers, leaves, or sprigs pinched from herbs, cut heads of grain, cherries picked from mature trees, or hazelnuts gleaned from the ground. Then we will see how love bears fruit, both to nourish us and to give new life.

———

*Julian of Norwich, *Revelations of Divine Love*. Ed. Barry Windeatt (Oxford: Oxford University Press, 2015), 45.

The Daily Reality of Returning

Returning to God is a daily reality for every Christian. As we turn our faces to God, we can be like a young toddler hard at play, who turns every few minutes to look at his mother or father to share a smile, seek guidance, ask for help, or find forgiveness. The child looks to his parent for the solid footing of a loving relationship, and we look to God for the same reasons.

Gratefulness turns our faces back to God. We feel grateful during a moment of silence in our day when we can finally stop and breathe for a moment or during a lively conversation when with a flash of connection we clearly see God's Image in the face of another human person. Natural beauty can awaken gratitude as we wonder at a gray mountain partially hidden by clouds or a shifting sea of yellow prairie grass, as we watch a many-colored sunset or count the stars, as we see a work of art, or as we hear the laughter of a child.

We also spin our faces back toward God when we come to our limits. When we are faced with a tough decision and we can't tell which way to go. When we fall down and have run out of strength to pull ourselves up and dust ourselves off. When we know that we are just going to fall down again and we can't imagine a world in which things will work out to be okay. When our pain becomes unbearable. Or when we must let go of a person or project we love because we know we can't shelter, protect, and control the world around us. In these moments, we turn back toward God for help. We look to God and ask: Are you still here? Do you still care? What are you going to do about this?

It is not always easy to look to God. We may be shy, we may be angry, or we may be burning with shame. We may look around us and realize God has left us alone in the room and we are met only with dark and cold fear. Fear grabs us with physical force—our hearts pump, our hands go cold, our stomachs churn.

We can turn to God, even in times of anger, shame, or fear, only when we think about our relationship with God as a relationship built by love.

That probably sounds appalling and weak to the wailing child left alone in a room. How can some vague sense of love match the cruel world of injustice, danger, or abandonment?

But the love that a parent shares with his or her child is a lot more than just an idea or fuzzy feeling. Their love is a relationship of mutual trust and vulnerability built up over time. It started with physical care. The parent—however imperfectly—responded to the needs of the infant for food, cleanliness, warmth, and sensory stimulation (through loving words, familiar smells and tastes, eye contact, and gentle touch). It continued as the parent provided healthy boundaries to keep the child safe as he explored the world, comforted his pains, and taught him by telling stories, sharing jokes, laughing, and playing together. The child who has this kind of strong attachment with his parent knows that even if the parent has left for a moment, no matter how that makes him feel, Daddy or Mommy will come back. That child trusts the parent, even when he's left in a vulnerable situation, because his parent has proven her love.

If God's perfect love is like a parent's love, we may at times be left by ourselves in fear, failure, or pain, but we are never left without the relationship—the evidence of God's love. If we look back into our lives, we will always find it. If we search for God, we will find God, sometimes where we least expect. This kind of daily returning may be the type of thing the Lord was referring to when God said returning could be our salvation.

Set your table

As you sit down to eat dinner, set the table. No matter what's on the menu, or if the idea of a "menu" is laughable. Even if you are scooping take out noodles from a Styrofoam container to a paper plate or setting out plastic silverware on the table at a fast-food restaurant. You need to eat. Do it with a plate, a fork, a spoon, a knife, a napkin, and a glass of water. If you're feeling fancy, add a placemat or a tablecloth. Leave your cell phone and tablet somewhere out of sight. Turn off the TV. Sit down. Preferably with someone else. Give God thanks for what you are eating. Take note of the everyday miracle that you have food to eat, food that a farmer has planted and harvested, a truck driver has stacked and shipped, a grocer has bought and sold, a cook—perhaps you, a loved one, or a minimum wage worker—has prepared and heated, and a server has placed in front of you. Setting the table is just one way of acknowledging the miracle.

Notice how it feels for you to set your place.

Setting a place for myself to eat at the table feels at the same time both familiar and foreign to me. Familiar because setting the table was one of my daily chores throughout childhood. I shared this job with my brother and sister. Every night one of us put down dinner plates for each member of the family. To the left of the plate was a fork, to the right of the plate—at our dominant hand—were a knife, blade facing toward your own plate (and not toward your neighbors—tradition has it that back in the day when knives were sharper and where you pointed your blade mattered, this was less aggressive to the person sitting next to you), and a spoon on a folded paper napkin. At the tip of the knife, we placed a glass of water or milk. Since my Grandpa Glenn was a Wisconsin farmer, no meal was complete without skimmed milk, preferably from a Jersey cow. Often we set a smaller plate above the fork for bread or salad, and a small bowl for canned fruit. My mother brought foods from the kitchen in serving bowls, which rested on hot pads or trivets. We often lit candles. Then our family sat down together to eat.

Our time together was not idyllic. That long, dark-stained wood dining table with claw feet was surrounded by loud, emotional, picky, needy human beings, but we were together. And if the meal resulted in someone shouting or storming off with their plate to slam their bedroom door, at least we had set the table as a gesture of kindness to one another.

Despite my history, setting the table feels foreign to me now because I have two young children ages four and two. The set table is a dim memory of a cozy distant past for me. Family mealtimes are much less structured for Clint, me, and our two preschool daughters. Most days I've been in such a rush that when I finish cooking, I serve the food directly from the stove or microwave to plates that come from the cabinet and that go straight to the table with whatever utensil can be used to shovel that food into my daughters' mouths. Dinner can be a whirl of "I want milk!" and "I need a fork!" and "I'm still hungry." I feel lucky on the days when I finally get to sit down and eat! At which point my daughters, bored with the food on their own plates, will come sit in my lap and eat the food from my plate. When we finish, there is food on the floor, on the furniture, in my hair, smeared into my clothes.

Other days I eat standing at the counter. Or I eat a banana and a protein bar on the run. No grateful forethought, no gracious setting down to prompt me to stop to think about where my food had come from, how it had gotten to me, or how it will make me feel later.

At the beginning, God gave human beings one job. In one place the Creator calls this job "to rule over the earth," a little later "to work and take care of" a garden (Genesis 1:28, 2:15).

In these commands, God gave us *humans*, creatures fashioned out of rich garden dirt called *humus*, one task: to attend. As we attend, we remember our humble origins and stretch toward the earth we were made from, we are present to its needs for protection and care, and then we serve God by attending those needs with gratefulness. The heart of this task is the daily, often grueling, work of finding food for ourselves and for those we love, of tending to the rhythms of life in the garden, the field, and the city. Though this work can be painful and though it is almost always hard, it can also be good for our souls. This work is the reality God has made for the good of our souls, the path created to lead us to the one who sustains us by love.

What we eat and how we get that food can be a major struggle in our world today. But don't stress. Just give attention. Set out plates and utensils on your table. Wonder at the fact that you have food to meet your body's needs. Let your table become a special place for a humble meal. Enjoy. As Wendell Berry puts it, in the pleasure of eating "we experience and celebrate our dependence and gratitude, for we are living from mystery, from creatures we did not make and powers we cannot comprehend."* You may realize that, without intending to, you have set a place for God.

———

*Wendell Berry, "The Pleasures of Eating," *What Are People For?* (Berkeley, CA: Counterpoint, 2010), 152.

Sing a hymn or a lullaby—out loud

When I was a child, my mother used to break into song at the most inappropriate moments. She would belt out her version of a song so unexpectedly, with so much energy and excitement, that it often startled me out of a bad mood and set a better tone for my day. As a preteen, I rolled my eyes a lot at her singing voice and her forgetfulness about the "real" words to the songs, but Mom just kept on singing.

Many years later, when I had my own baby girl, I was surprised how easily Mom's songs came back to me. While the baby watched wide-eyed from her bouncy chair, I'd find myself alone in my apartment putting those high school singing lessons Mom paid for to good use with a rousing tune: I'd belt out "Oh, What a Beautiful Morning" from the musical *Oklahoma!*, then I'd take a deep breath and break into Johnny Appleseed's "Oh, the Lord's Been Good to Me." My mom had given me a good set of keys for unlocking problems and getting around the obstacles of life.

Then, for a long time, I lost those keys.

I didn't even notice they were gone. I was too busy. My mental energy those days went to all the *stuff* that had to be done: laundry, diapers, food, sleep, friendships, church, volunteering, and start again tomorrow. I worked hard to ignore it, but I was also in physical pain from overwork and lack of self-care, and I didn't know what to do or how to change.

Singing a cheerful song seemed like putting a coat of bright paint over the weariness that made my days heavy and gray. The rain of negative thinking washed it off before it even had a chance to dry. Most songs just made me cry.

I did sing a few hymns and lullabies with my little girl before she went to sleep. I couldn't remember very many, but we had a few in rotation and she would request her favorites.

One night when she was about two, she sat up in my lap and got excited. "Figgin pon it," she said, "Sing figgin pon it."

I wracked my brain. What in the world was she talking about? I tried a bunch of songs. She shook her head no. I tried the old hymn "Come Thou Fount."

> *Come thou fount of every blessing,*
> *Tune my heart to sing thy grace,*
> *Streams of mercy never ceasing,*
> *Call for songs of loudest praise,*
> *Sing me some melodious sonnet,*
> *Sung by flaming tongues above,*

I was almost all the way through the song before she finally nodded and relaxed into my arms.

> *Praise the name, I'm fixed upon it*
> *Name of thy redeeming love.*

Fixed upon it! For her, this song was summed up in that line. She was fixed on the name of love. As my daughter's tiny body lay back onto me, my weary broken heart relaxed, too.

I leaned back into God's arms, turned, and looked up into my loving Parent's face, and saw there so much love. More than I had guessed or expected for one "prone to wander" as the next verse says. A hymn I had known for years still held new riches for me.

Our voices are instruments we carry around all day, every day. Good days and bad, happy and sad, as my mom says. We have off-days when we don't feel like singing, or when we wish we knew a good lament song to let out the groan that weighs inside. But we also carry a hidden depth of knowledge in old, unused, nearly forgotten songs.

Songs have long been a powerful memory store. Songs help us learn about the world as young children: letters, numbers, and games. Hymnals use song to help us learn and remember theology. When I was a frazzled new Spanish teacher in that windowless inner-city classroom, I discovered songs that could help my students learn new Spanish vocabulary and cultural concepts. Singing completely recharged my classroom. When we started singing, I started having fun. My students started having fun. They sang in Spanish in class, in the hallway, at home. They complained to me that they heard others singing our songs outside class using *the wrong words*. Their parents were amazed to hear them using Spanish. Visitors to our building stopped outside my classroom door amazed to hear the kids enjoying Spanish. I didn't have any special powers as a teacher, but together we had song. Song put Spanish in their bones.

Singing is powerful in even the darkest of places. In the strange story of Acts 16, the apostle Paul and his friend Silas were put in jail for freeing a young enslaved girl from spiritual oppression. Messing with other people's human property was a serious offense, so Paul and Silas were stripped, beaten, *then* (according to the passage) severely whipped and thrown into prison. The jailer was given careful instructions not to let them escape. He put them in the inner cell and put their feet in stocks.

Acts records what happened next with economy and precision:

> About midnight Paul and Silas were praying and singing hymns to God, and the other prisoners were listening to them. Suddenly there was such a violent earthquake that the foundations of the prison were shaken. At once all the prison doors flew open, and everyone's chains came loose. The jailer woke up, and when he saw the prison doors open, he drew his sword and was about to kill himself because he thought the prisoners had escaped. But Paul shouted, "Don't harm yourself! We are all here!"
>
> The jailer called for lights, rushed in and fell trembling before Paul and Silas. He then brought them out and asked, "Sirs, what must I do to be saved?" (Acts 16:25–30 NIV)

It would be an exaggeration to say that Paul and Silas's song created that earthquake. But it certainly helped them cope with a difficult situation. When the doors came flying open, those men didn't spring right up and run out. They had already transformed their prison cell into a place of worship, and they weren't ready to leave yet. That attitude saved a man's life. In that way singing does have the power to rattle prison doors and iron fetters in your life. It can turn your face back to God on the hardest days, and it can save your life and the lives of others.

You don't have to sing cheerful songs or Jesus songs. Try different ones. Remember songs you haven't sung in forever. Even if they are goofy kids' songs. Or old hymns that you have to look up the words to online. Or the cheesy repetitive choruses from youth group that made you cringe. Or pop music. God loves a good pop song! God also loves flamenco, jazz, blues, rap, gospel. He loves marching songs and Broadway tunes born out of life's joy and angry, aching laments born out of slavery, imprisonment, and loss. Learn a new song. Look up the words to an old one. Find your own songs. Make one up if you have to.

Whichever song you choose, don't just listen to others sing it on your iPod or music app or YouTube. Breathe life into that song yourself. Let the music come out of your throat and your mouth. Use your time in the shower to sing your song. Belt out a tune while you vacuum or clean. Hide in a dark closet. Let loose your lyrics. Sing with a child. Let your body get into it. (Or not.)

Fill your lungs to bursting next to God—who is your very breath, your audience, and your duet partner—and sing.

Hand over your worries before bed

When I was a teenager, I spent an embarrassing amount of my life thinking about time. Quite the budding philosopher, I stubbornly preferred using a round-faced analog clock that ticked and whirled its hands, rather than a digital clock with blinking numbers. With the analog clock I could *see* the time passing, like a physical distance, concrete and measurable. I wondered: If every second and minute and hour on the clock is an objective measure, why does our experience of time speed up and slow down? And I contemplated how each moment of time that we pass through is, proportionally, a smaller part of our whole life. So for a two-year-old, a year seems eternal, half a lifetime, but for even a thirty-year-old, a year can feel like it is gone before you know it, because a year is only a tiny fraction of the whole life experience.

Time moves quickly and mysteriously and yet its passage can weigh heavily on us. Every day we have new experiences and new challenges. Things happen to us that have never happened before and may or may not ever happen again, filling our lives and our minds to overflowing every single day.

We often come to the end of the day carrying many unresolved concerns—people to interact with or care for, e-mails to write, work that sometimes succeeds and sometimes fails, appointments to make. If we came through the day without any major catastrophes, we probably still have news that others are suffering. Our own struggles seem small in comparison, but our minds replay our particular experiences and decisions as we toss and turn on our pillows: Did we do right? Did we do wrong? What will we do tomorrow?

When Oprah asked comedian Stephen Colbert to name his favorite verse in the Bible he didn't miss a beat. Paraphrasing Matthew 6:27, Colbert takes comfort in the fact that when Jesus told us, "So I say to you do not worry, for who among you by worrying can change a hair on his head, or add a cubit to the span of his life," that was a command. Not a suggestion. Worry doesn't get us anywhere. But it is one thing to say, "*Stop worrying!*" and another to actually break free from worry.

As a quiet act of self-care, sit on the edge of your bed for a few minutes before you go to sleep and hand your worried thoughts to God one by one.

This daily habit dates back to at least the Middle Ages, when wandering monk Ignatius Loyola wrote down a five-step version of it he called the "Daily Examen." He set it as a kind of pop quiz to stop and notice where God was present in his life each day. I first came across this simpler version in a little book called *The Gift of Being Yourself* by David G. Benner.

As you come to bed, look for moments where God felt present or absent from your life. Replay the mental tape of your day and invite God to watch with you. Or think of the past twenty-four hours as a backpack you are unpacking and consider each major event as you bring it out of the bag and hold it in your hands. As you reflect, notice what you feel with compassion for yourself. It's okay to be you, to feel what you feel. It was so hard when you came against a boundary that you couldn't get past. It was fantastic when you responded with patience you didn't know you had in you. It was sad when unkind words slipped out a moment later. But try not to make judgments about your actions or get caught up in regret. We are digging deeper in the bag here, looking for something else.

Some of the memories and feelings will be negative. Ignatius calls this desolation. These are moments when we feel that God has abandoned us. Allow yourself to notice your shame, your embarrassment, your fear, your anger, your disgust, or your inadequacy and consider how you responded to those emotions during the day. Once you have remembered the experience and acknowledged to yourself how you felt, turn your face to God. Hand the memory over to the One who sees, the One who was there.

Not all your memories of your day will be negative. Dwell for a few moments on the joys of your life today and the times when God felt near. Ignatius calls these consolation. A friend said a kind word. You laughed at a cheesy joke. You enjoyed a peaceful moment, ate great food, or a read a challenging book. You made time to delight in a loved one. You accomplished a goal that you have aimed toward for a long time, you helped an elderly man count change at a checkout counter, or you asked for forgiveness and your friend assured you that you were forgiven. God was there, too. Hand over those memories. Ask yourself also what you have to be thankful for. Thank God for them as you roll them into your Savior's outstretched hand.

You do not need to spend an hour at this, or even half an hour. Just a few minutes will do, and set yourself a timer if that will help you give your full attention. Every day there will be desolations and consolations, feelings of cold abandonment and warm presence. Some days will be harder and the scales will tip toward desolation. Other days will be light and full of consolation. But the point of this practice is to learn to see that no matter how we *feel* at any given time, no matter whether it makes the most "rational" sense in any given moment or whether we can imagine God's presence vividly, God is here. God is present in all of our lives as the one who sees us and knows us and has compassion on us.

This exercise of our memories can help smooth out the uneven experience of time that troubled me as a young person. We can look back at experiences when we felt satisfied and joyful—surely God was there!—and experience now shame and desolation at sins or mistakes we had overlooked. We can look back on experiences that seemed to be times of total abandonment, and experience now how God was present with us the whole time. Or we can feel a confirmation that our impressions at the time made sense. But by remembering, inviting God to be present with us as we remember, and handing over the memories to the God who cares for us, we gain freedom from the worries (troubling experiences or ideal delights) of the past. We do not have to carry them forward into the present and the future.

Just outside Saint Louis, Missouri, there is a hotel where the staff place their Gideon Bibles open on the nightstand, instead of banished to the rarely opened nightstand drawer.

When I stayed there and noticed the book, I leaned in toward it, curious about the yellow highlighted words from Psalm 4:8 laid out for me with such care. "In peace I will both lie down and sleep," it read, "for you alone, O LORD, make me to dwell in safety" (NASB).

Unpack your weary mind, reach out, and hand over your thoughts to God then, hopefully, lie down to sleep at peace.

Blood and Tar at the Altar

The first move in right relationship with God is when we lift our shy, fallen faces to seek God's face—to look into God's eyes and accept the gift and invitation of love. God has already done the work of salvation in our lives. All we have to do is look to God. When I was a child growing up in a Southern Baptist church, this happened most often when we sang heartfelt hymns at the end of the sermon, songs about coming home just as we are. We went forward and knelt on the carpeted red steps at the front of the sanctuary. We cried and we prayed right there in front of everybody, and somebody was always ready with a box of tissues. And we didn't even mind that everybody was looking because we were looking God in the face. Jesus was all we could see. Now, as an adult, I have stumbled up a different aisle to a different type of altar and found God.

A few years ago, the Anglican bishop in our area, a gentle, unpretentious man, came to our small local church dressed in his white robes with red trim, carrying a shepherd's crosier and wearing a gold embroidered miter on his head. As I knelt before him, he laid his hands on my head, prayed for me, and confirmed me as an Anglican Christian. My husband was also confirmed, along with two young men he had mentored, a college student, and some others. We had all been baptized and had learned the basic beliefs of the church and we were looking for a formal *confirmation* in our lives of faith—a chance to receive God's grace again the way I did at my baptism as a seven-year-old child and to look out at God's people and say, "I still believe."

That Sunday morning was an important moment in my life of faith: a moment when I returned to God. This would probably surprise you if you knew me in those days, because I worked hard for the church, and from the outside, things mostly looked like they were going okay. My husband and I were youth pastors with theological education, I helped lead a women's Bible study, and I had many friendships with the other young mothers.

But as we turned our car into the church parking lot before the confirmation service that July morning, I told Clint, "I had hoped that I would feel different today, but lately I just feel covered in my own sin, as though it is a sticky tar that I just can't get off." I longed to feel a rush of joy as I committed myself to our church community, but I just felt heavy. I had hoped this day would be a mountaintop experience with a feeling of fireworks and an overwhelming sense of God's presence, but so far it was neither. I knew that my reality in Christ was one of forgiveness, but I couldn't feel anything but guilt and shame. I felt overcome by the fact that I had made several big and painful mistakes recently; I had sought refuge in my own efforts and other distractions. I was too much. I was not enough.

"What does God even see in me?" I wondered.

When it came my turn that morning, I knelt before the

bishop with my head low. The bishop laid his hands on my head and prayed words of blessing over me in the strange, old language of the Book of Common Prayer:

> DEFEND, O Lord, thy Servant Laura with thy heavenly grace, that she may continue thine forever, and daily increase in thy Holy Spirit, more and more, until she come unto thy everlasting kingdom. Amen.*

Then, as he had warned us he would, the bishop paused for a moment to listen to God. Not all bishops do this, but our bishop likes to. His fingers trembled a little on my hair. I knelt there with my eyes closed, breathing in and out slowly, and nothing mystical happened. When I opened my eyes and stood up, the room felt bright. A cloud that covered the sun that morning blew out of the way, and sunlight beamed through a skylight, leaving a sharp white shape on the floor. That was all.

Clint and I rushed off to lead the youth meeting.

When we came back to the sanctuary for the communion service, we were only just in time for my favorite prayer. We knelt and prayed together with our church family:

> We do not presume to come to this thy Table, O most merciful Lord, trusting in our own righteousness, but in thy manifold and great mercies. We are not worthy so much as to gather up the crumbs under thy Table. But thou art the same Lord, whose property is always to have mercy. Grant us, therefore, gracious Lord, so to

eat the flesh of thy dear Son Jesus Christ, and to drink
his blood, that our sinful bodies may be made clean by
his body, and our souls washed by his most precious
blood and that we may evermore dwell in him and he
in us. Amen.*

The odd prayers and practices of the Anglican Book
of Common Prayer often seem to come from a different world entirely. They startle every single one of my
twenty-first-century sensibilities as they matter-of-factly
ask me to repeat week after week these bizarre words about
eating flesh and drinking blood. What am I? A dog licking
crumbs under a table? A cannibal and a vampire? How in
the world can sinful bodies be made clean by Christ's body?
And why do Christians keep talking about being washed in
blood? As a child, I sang hymns about fountains filled with
blood, and now here I was as an adult praying that blood
would wash my soul. The horrific violence of the whole thing
made my stomach churn.

But I love the Book of Common Prayer exactly because
these weird old prayers never cease to startle me out of my
boredom and preoccupation. They bring my attention to the
blind spots I have developed from living here and now. They
connect me to a church, a Body of Christ, older, more global,
and more challenging than I ever imagined possible. They
teach me how to give God my full, undivided attention.

I went to the communion rail silent that morning, thinking. Christian life is not about glory in the ways I like to think
of it. No mystical visions and special attentions from God

today. No gifts of tears or soaring emotions. No glossy photos of picture-perfect faith. Just glory Jesus-style. As Eugene Peterson puts it, "The bright presence of God backlighting what the world despises or ignores."† Dirt. Depression. Illness. Invisibility. Exhaustion. Misunderstanding. And God's presence.

We prayed, back in our seats, "And here, we offer and present unto thee, O Lord, ourselves, our souls and bodies, to be a reasonable, holy and living sacrifice unto thee…"* more blood, more gore. Now it was my own body on the altar.

The bishop found me in the church gym after the service. He told me that with his hands on my head that morning, as he listened to God, he received no special thought or word from God. Instead, he had only a feeling. He felt overwhelmed to the point of trembling with a sense of God's love for me.

Love? For *me?* The sin-smeared? The doubt-filled? The angry? The fearful? The imperfect? The ashamed? *Love?* And why couldn't *I* feel that love?

Why am I squeamish about Jesus's sacrifice? What is it about blood that makes me so uncomfortable? A person's lifeblood belongs hidden, nourishing their own body. Jesus's blood was poured out. As a gift freely given, at great cost. Gerhard Von Rad writes: "According to the Old Testament view, blood and life belong to God alone; wherever a man commits murder he attacks God's very own right of possession. To destroy life goes far beyond man's proper sphere. Spilled blood cannot be shoveled underground; it cries aloud to heaven and complains directly to the Lord of life. In this statement that dismal, primitive feeling of shuddering before spilled blood is wonderfully combined with the most genuine and mature faith in God as the protector and guardian of life."‡

God knew the one solvent that could wash away the sticky tar of my sin. It was not what I wanted, not what I expected, not what made sense to me. But what I needed more than anything. What if it was love?

Returning looks different for each of us at different points in our journeys. Altar calls, prayer with friends, wrestling with God alone, yelling in God's face. That morning—for me—returning to God looked like a church service full of sixteenth-century prayers, a bishop's touch, and eyes squinted at the brightness. It looked like taking God's poured out blood seriously, with amazement.

What does returning look like to you?

---

*The General Synod of the Anglican Church of Canada, "The Order for the Ministration of Holy Communion," *Book of Common Prayer Canada* (Toronto: Anglican Book Centre, 1962), 83–84.

†Eugene H. Peterson, *Christ Plays in Ten Thousand Places: A Conversation in Spiritual Theology* (Grand Rapids, MI: William B. Eerdmans, 2005), 103.

‡Gerhard Von Rad, *Genesis: A Commentary*. Trans. John H. Marks (London: SCM Press, 1961), 102–3.

Clean up a mess

Dirt is the unavoidable reality we live in. When left to themselves, our bodies, clothes, homes, and cars all get dirtier and dirtier. The dishes and utensils that we set on the table become smeared with food. The white shirt we wore once gets smudged. The dust and grime of use or lack of use eventually settle on everything. And the grind of washing up never seems to end. The sun rises, the sun sets, time presses on, and always another blessed shirt, counter, tabletop, plate, or surface needs cleaning.

My approach to cleaning is to ignore a mess until I can't ignore it anymore then get it over with. I secretly hope that fairies will come and take care of my dirty business while I sleep. If I can get someone else to clean for me by neglect, trickery, or payment, I will. I don't get a lot of pleasure out of washing up. I'd rather be reading a book, scrolling through social media feeds, playing with my kids, or doing something fun or "useful to society."

This attitude sustained me pretty well through my twenties. My husband and I didn't make huge messes. We were busy and didn't mind a little dust along the baseboards or soap scum in the bathtub. When it got bad—when we ran out of dishes or clean underwear, or when we had time—we cleaned up.

Then I had a child. Within two weeks I was appalled by

how much laundry, how many dishes, and how much overall mess one very tiny person with very tiny clothes could cause. Once my mother left, absolutely no fairies arrived to clean for me. My husband was still in school full-time *and* working three jobs to make ends meet. We couldn't afford hired help. I was confused about how to stay on top of the mess, jealous that Clint could leave our messy home behind every day, embarrassed at my failure, and bitter at the drudgery of cleaning up.

I considered myself a feminist, meaning that I planned to pursue "meaningful work" outside our home throughout my childbearing years. I never imagined myself stuck at home day in and day out, wiping faces, bodies, tables, and floors and keeping house.

New York Times columnist Ross Douthat describes well why many young professionals are tempted to uncharacteristic whining when they have children. We have been used to almost complete freedom from permanent commitment and "it inspires a ferocious shock when a child arrives and that oh-so-modern lifestyle gives way to challenges that seem almost medieval, and duties that seem impossibly absolute."* I like that description, "almost medieval" because the Middle Ages were nothing if not very physical. I have a mental stereotype of grungy serfs doing drudgery work on a feudal farm. We are tempted to think of this medieval reality as backward and unenlightened, their work as meaningless and inhumane, yet today a thousand years later, dirt still challenges us.

We have come so far—why do we still have to clean up?

You may groan to hear it, but the dull daily work of

cleaning up is one of the best ways to stretch toward God. If you want to live a life of attention to the God who attends to you, drudgery has the power to stop our preoccupation with ourselves and show us God.

Kathleen Norris puts it well: "Is it not a good joke that when God gave us work to do as a punishment for our disobedience in Eden, it was work that can never be finished, but only repeated, day in and day out, season upon season, year after year? I see here not only God's keen sense of humor, but also a creative and zestful love. It is precisely these thankless, boring, repetitive tasks that are the hardest for the workaholic or utilitarian mind to appreciate, and God knows that being rendered temporarily mindless as we toil is what allows us to approach the temple of holy leisure."[†]

Norris goes on to say, "When confronting a sinkful of dirty dishes—something I do regularly as my husband is the cook in our house and I am the dishwasher—I admit that I generally lose sight of the fact that God is inviting me to play. But I recall that as a college student I sometimes worked as a teacher's aide in a kindergarten and was interested to note that one of the most popular play areas for both boys and girls was a sink in the corner of the room."[†]

Norris describes that what the children at the play sink enjoyed was the sensory experience, the tickle of warm and cool water on the skin, bubbles rising from suds, acts of filling and pouring, dishes floating and sinking. My own young daughters find delight at the sink multiple times a day, hands, faces, whole bodies in the water, squealing with delight.

That is *not* how I feel when I begin to wash dishes, do the laundry, or scrub the floor. I can be really immature about it, too. I am irritated that what I just cleaned needs cleaning again. I feel grossed out by dirt or food on my hands. I moan and complain. And yet by the end of the task, when I stand back to see what I've done, I usually find that work itself was the remedy my soul needed. I was part of the breathtaking miracle of making dirty things clean.

This stretch toward God means tackling a quiet good deed you already have to do. Wash those dishes in the sink. Scrub that spot from your favorite sweater. Throw some clothes in the washing machine. Fill a bucket with warm soapy water and dust baseboards or wipe the dashboard of your car. Feel the warm water on your hands with wonder, bordering on playfulness. Stand back and admire for a moment the accomplishment.

God makes all things new and makes dirty things clean. Even us.

————

*Ross Douthat, "Parental Pity Party," *New York Times*, Feb. 15, 2014.

†Kathleen Norris, *The Quotidian Mysteries: Laundry, Liturgy and "Women's Work"* (New York: Paulist Press, 1998), 26–27.

Ask someone for forgiveness

Christian writer and speaker Patsy Clairmont has said that apologizing gives her flu-like symptoms, and I feel the same way. I know it in the pit of my stomach the instant that I've done wrong: careless, unkind words slipped from my lips, I laughed at exactly the wrong moment, I selfishly took a small thing that didn't really belong to me, or I promised a friend I would help and *I totally forgot*. But even when I know clearly that I made a mistake, something deep inside me finds it physically unpleasant to admit that I am wrong. My body commits mutiny. My palms get sweaty. My legs get shaky. My eyes can look anywhere except the person's face. Like Adam and Eve in the garden, I am suddenly willing to try anything to get out of facing up to what I've done. I run away, hide, or try to cover up what I did. I become a sudden professional at explaining why it was that I did what I did in a nervous torrent of language, casting blame or otherwise trying to "help people see it from my perspective."

The word *confront*, like the word *attend*, comes from a Latin root. It means literally, "to meet face-to-face." To confront, though, is not a gentle face-to-face meeting between people at peace. It describes the unpleasant side of face-to-face relationship in this world. Human persons hurt one another—by accident, on purpose, or a mixture of both. When we do, the hardest thing in the world is to turn our faces toward one another and give one another our full attention. Suddenly, tilting our ears, focusing our eyes, turning our hearts toward one another is like trying to press the positive poles of two strong magnets together or touching two live wires to create sparks.

If there is one thing that can begin to dispel all the negative physical energy that builds up between two hurting and hurtful human beings, it is a good apology. But like gardening, I'm not that great at apologizing. When I realize I've made a mistake, shame immediately whispers lies that become a loop in my mind: "See, I told you that you are worthless and stupid. You'll never get anything right. No one will like you now. You are a bad friend and a bad person." I lose all nerve. The truth is that it takes a lot of courage and strength to apologize when we've done wrong. But the good news is that if we don't have that strength, we can build it up by practice.

Choose a small offense that you can adequately address in a few minutes. This is not the time to deal with the friend who hasn't spoken with you for six months or the family member who deserves more than a five-minute apology from you. Those are important, but what I'm imagining here is that we'll start smaller. Think of a coworker, a roommate, a member of your immediate family, a person you see daily and have a pretty good relationship with, but who you hurt recently in a small way. We all do it.

Take a moment by yourself before you apologize. Admit to yourself what you did and take responsibility for it. Look at it full on and see it for the ugly weed it is. Try to dig down to the root of why you did it, not to rationalize or make excuses but to understand yourself a little better and prevent it from happening again. Maybe you need to start by forgiving the person, because they hurt you, too, or forgiving yourself for making a mistake. Giving yourself this moment of space will help you to make a genuine apology, not one that seeks to smooth over a problem and keep people happy with you, but one that comes from your heart and digs out the rotten roots of sin in your life.

The words in the Old and New Testaments for *sin* mean literally "to miss the mark." Think of an arrow aimed at a target that flies from the bow, but falls short or to the side and fails to hit the goal. The aim of life is right-relatedness, the ability to live at peace with God and with others, to live side-by-side and face-to-face without shame or guilt. Sin comes in when we decide that living in peace and right relationship isn't in our best interests anymore. Peace starts to get itchy. We grow distracted by our own needs and desires and we fail to give our full attention.

It can take us by surprise that we have done something truly wrong when that was never our intention. We had our reasons, it made sense at the time, and so on and so forth. But we need to take that surprise as an invitation to give attention to our own pain and the pain we have caused others.

Apologizing, even when it means an uncomfortable face-to-face encounter, seeks to uproot the basic problem of our sin: We became distracted by selfish desires and inattentive to the needs of others. So, once you are ready to apologize, contact the person in the most personal way you can. Coming face-to-face the first time you see them after the offense (or the first time after you've resolved to apologize) is the best way. Be gentle with yourself and with the other person. If you are in a public place, invite them to come aside privately. If you won't see them for a long time, a phone call or a mailed handwritten letter are better than an e-mail or text message.

State what you did and take responsibility for it by saying, "What I did was wrong." Then say, "I'm sorry." State that you are not going to do it again. And say that you'd like to try to make up for what you did.

It will be awkward to look this person in the face and ask for forgiveness, and you may say the wrong thing. But a face-to-face encounter will show you where you stand with the person. Your relief will be palpable if he or she responds with genuine forgiveness. And if not, that will be clear, too. They may need time. What you did or said or failed to do has broken their trust. Rebuilding it will take time and work for both of you. But you have made a start.

When we admit to someone we have wronged that we messed up, it forces us to see things from God's perspective, beyond the boundaries of our own hurt. We rely on the reality of God's forgiveness. When we turn away from the wrong we have done and turn to God, our gentle Judge's response is always one of love and acceptance. Our wrongs have hurt others and cost God deeply in Jesus's death on the cross, but God eagerly waits to look us in the face again. Our loved ones do, too. Make it right.

Turning Toward Love

Love bade me welcome: yet my soul drew back,
Guilty of dust and sin.
But quick-eyed Love, observing me grow slack
From my first entrance in,
Drew nearer to me, sweetly questioning
If I lacked anything.

"A guest," I answered, "worthy to be here":
Love said, "You shall be he."
"I, the unkind, ungrateful? Ah my dear,
I cannot look on thee."
Love took my hand and smiling did reply,
"Who made the eyes but I?"

"Truth, Lord; but I have marred them; let my shame
Go where it doth deserve."
"And know you not," says Love, "who bore the blame?"
"My dear, then I will serve."
"You must sit down," says Love, "and taste my meat."
So I did sit and eat.

—George Herbert, "Love (III)"

Two parts of the definition of the word *attend* teach us

specifically how God stretches toward us in love, and how we can stretch toward God. First, *to attend* means simply "to be present." We attend class; we attend a business conference. Silent, still, watching, learning, receiving. In this stage, in the words of Eugene Peterson, "We deliberately interrupt our preoccupation with ourselves and attend to God, place ourselves intentionally in sacred space, in sacred time, in the holy presence—and wait."* The first part of building an attentive relationship with God is showing up.

However, to attend is not a passive act. It also means to serve. It means that we wait in a physical posture ready to spring into action. A priest attends at the altar of God, a doctor attends at the bedside of her patient, a courtier attends to the needs of his king, a waiter attends to his customers' tables, and a businesswoman attends to her business. When we place ourselves in God's presence and give our full attention, we will often be inspired to *do* a quiet good deed: to meet a need or desire, to solve a problem or to seek the best outcome in a situation. Not for our own sakes, but genuinely for the sake of another.

Attentiveness is a humble posture. In our relationship with God, we receive and we offer, but the gift always begins with God. We accept the grace that God offers us, grace that startles and confuses us, that demands our complete attention. As we stretch toward God's gifts even in our routine daily existence—life, creation, relationship—we lay aside our other thoughts, plans, and intentions, and with open hands and ready service, we offer back up to God everything that God has given. Attentiveness, both to wait and to serve, is the posture of thankfulness. Attentiveness is love.

----

*Eugene Peterson, *Christ Plays in Ten Thousand Places: A Conversation in Spiritual Theology* (Grand Rapids, MI: William B. Eerdmans, 2005), 41.

Send a handwritten note to a friend

When I write a handwritten letter, I sit down at the small, dark oak desk I have used since I was a child and pull out the deep drawer on the left where I keep a random assortment of stationery, cards, and special paper. I come to the desk with a specific person on my mind, usually a friend or a family member who I am separated from by many miles. A person who I like or love or just generally care about, and who is far away, beyond my ability to see a face, hear a voice, touch a hand, or lean in to hug and kiss. I miss that person and I want to express that to her. I recall the latest bit of juicy news I heard from him or a recent sadness, and so I sit down at my desk and I wonder how they are doing.

It is this wondering that drives me as I riffle around in my drawer and settle on a card or piece of paper. In that moment, I want to be connected to this person. I understand that their presence in my life is a gift and that no matter who they are, their face reflects Christ's, so I stop what I am doing and come here to give my attention to that gift.

I choose a pen, but I know that whether I use a green gel pen or a black ballpoint or even a pencil, my choice is less important than the words I choose. I squint my eyes for a moment, wrinkling my forehead as I think of what to say. This special paper won't give me much of a margin for error, so I slow down and think of my words carefully. Not too carefully—I have to make do with only a little time. I write a name at the top, then I remind myself of Lewis Carroll's tongue-in-cheek advice, "Don't fill more than a page and a half with apologies for not having written sooner."* I am not writing, primarily, to tell this person about myself, even how sorry I am. I am writing to let her know that she is not alone in the world. I am sitting here at my desk thinking of her and wondering about her body in the world: How did the surgery go? Is the new baby here yet? Is the project finished? What is spring like where you are? Are there figs on the trees this year? Has the weather changed yet? My friend Andrea learned from a little book called *Gift of a Letter* that the essence of every letter is: "Dear You, I am here thinking of you now."†

Despite that idyllic vision, letter writing makes me uncomfortable. I often try to avoid it, or in the busy space of daily life, I fail to make it a priority. I never write as many letters as I mean to write. I set myself lofty goals such as: "This year, I will send a Christmas card to fifty friends with a short personal note." And I plug away in a disorganized effort for a few days, or even weeks, before I give up. But I'm not just lazy or thoughtless, I'm afraid.

Writing a letter is an intimate act. As you write, you offer a man or a woman made in God's Image a gift of yourself, a physical token of your loving care that he or she can touch, hear, see, smell, and perhaps even taste. In the whole world, there is no other arrangement of those words in that order written down in your unique handwriting. A handwritten letter is a private, direct address to one person, tucked away from prying eyes into an envelope, sealed to make sure that they are the only one who sees it. No corporations mine it for marketing data and no other friends see it posted online. The beauty of the thing is shared between a small number of people at most. This secrecy makes personal letters the most honest and vulnerable form of writing, since they are usually written and read in solitude without editing, posturing, or looking one another in the face. It is easier to express an idea or opinion freely and abstractly as if it is a meeting of pure mind. John Donne says, "More than kisses letters mingle souls; for thus friends absent speak."[†] It is a lovely image, but soul-mingling is also intense. Perhaps our limits of time, effort, and resources naturally protect the fact that we cannot and should not write long intimate letters to everyone we know. Letters and their communication mission are also fragile. A letter between friends can heal and connect, but sloppy, rude, or irritating words can also wound and break relationships. In an era of instant communication, we must pause and examine our words. It is easier to share with the whole world, or at least a large group of friends or followers who may love you or hate you, than it is to really open up your heart to one person who could reject you.

When I finish my letter, when I sign it and seal it, address it and stamp it, then send it off to find its way to my friend's place in the world, I may never hear back even an acknowledgment that it arrived safely, that it was opened, or that it was read. But like all gifts from God, we give the gift of a letter freely, no strings attached.

Are you willing to take that risk? Stretch toward one

person in the world, think of where he is, or wonder how she might be doing. Write that person a handwritten note. Receive, notice, and appreciate the gift of friendship you have received and pass that gift along.

———

*Lewis Carroll, "Eight or Nine Wise Words about Letter-Writing" (Oxford: Emberlin and Son, 1890), 14.

†Angela Stoddard, *Gift of a Letter* (New York: Doubleday, 1990), 60.

‡John Donne, "To Sir Henry Wotton," *Poems of John Donne*, Vol. II. Ed. E. K. Chambers (London: Lawrence & Bullen, 1896), 7.

Admit your sins to God

As you go about your day, pause at some point to tell your Maker something you've done your own way recently. Follow the rules of a decent apology. No excuses. No explanations or rationalizations. No going back. Then wait a few minutes in the quiet and see how God responds.

Admitting my sins to God was not something I thought about regularly before I began attending an Anglican church. It was just kind of assumed that once you prayed to accept Jesus, all that was taken care of. No need to draw it out. But I didn't find that very satisfying. I was a shy, awkward kid, and I felt sensitive that I did wrong things all the time. So I felt like I carried my sins (and even the sins of others) around in a fog of shame, guilt, and pain. There's no good theological reason to feel like that as a Christian, but I did. I had no idea what to do about it.

When I first encountered the practice of confession from the Anglican Book of Common Prayer, I was young and living on my own in a big city. I wasn't much of a late-night partyer, but I had early mornings Monday to Friday and worked long days. Getting up on a Sunday morning to travel thirty minutes to church took some extra effort. But oddly enough, one thought would consistently jolt me out of my warm sheets those slow mornings, "If I'm late, I'll miss the prayer of confession." This prayer was the best thing about my new church.

Here is what we prayed at the beginning of the service most weeks, the prayer that got my lazy butt out of bed and into my padded seat in the rented space where our little church family met week after week, the prayer that drew my knees down onto the concrete floor:

> *Most merciful Father, we humbly admit that we need*
> *your help.*
> *We confess that we have wandered from your way like*
> *lost sheep;*
> *We have followed too much the devices and desires of*
> *our own hearts,*
> *and have failed to do what is right.*
> *You alone can save us.*
> *Have mercy upon us Lord;*
> *wipe out our sins and teach us to forgive others.*
> *Bring forth in us the fruit of the Spirit that we may live*
> *as disciples of Christ.*
> *This we ask in the name of Jesus our Savior. Amen.*

This prayer helped me to understand what my sin was: wandering from God's way and following my own. And it helped me to remember that there was nothing I could do to fix that on my own. It was God's grace through Christ that called me to turn my face back toward Jesus.

After we prayed, the minister said: "God has promised in his Word that when we confess our sins, he forgives us and cleanses us from all unrighteousness."

And we replied together in relief, "Thanks be to God."*

Those words were so good for me week after week. They took my sins seriously and their repetition reminded me of my reality in Christ: I was forgiven. God graciously accepted me. I carried no blame. I needed that reminder weekly. Is it odd for a girl raised adamantly Protestant to find so much relief in the confession of sins? Eastern Orthodox writer Alexander Schmemann points out that confession is a reaffirmation of our baptism.[†] When we confess our sins in the congregation of the church, a slender thread leads us back again and again, week after week, to the one-time event when God's grace washed us clean, when God's smile and pat on the back welcomed us into the family as water dripped down our faces.

Those Sundays when I hurried to church to confess, a long time had passed since my baptism. As a child in the Baptist church, I was baptized as soon as they would let me—seven years old. I was so tiny in the deep water of the baptistery high in the wall of the sanctuary to the left of the pulpit, I had to stand on a concrete block. My foot slipped when the pastor dunked me under, and I came up splashing and sputtering for air. In my child's mind, I was pretty sure I had nearly died (not that the pastor would have let me).

But though my baptism seemed important when it happened, time passed and I forgot about what happened that day. I came to the point where I wasn't sure anymore what kept me coming back to church. Why couldn't I just quit? What kept leading me back to the messy, broken body of Christ? But confessing my sins each week reminded me that every day is a gift of God's grace. A gift of the same grace that had washed over me like a wave, washed me clean, drowned me in the love of God, and washed me up on the shore of a brave new reality. My little death and resurrection. Each week I turned my face toward God again.

Reconnecting with God through confession, whether you make it to a church or only pray alone at home, washes us over again with a new wave from the ocean of this once-and-for-all grace. It keeps our hand on the thread. Keeps us returning. Reminds us that we are—all of us broken, shamefaced sinners—in this together.

On those Sunday mornings after confession, I rose from the cold concrete feeling a little lighter. I left the service knowing that God and I were okay. Not because I said some magic words of confession, but because, through those words, I had turned my hard heart to the One who washes me clean.

———

*John G. Mason, *A Liturgy for Today's Church*, prepared in consultation with others and authorized for use at Christ Church New York City. This particular confession and response are adapted and modernized from the Morning Prayer service in the English Book of Common Prayer published in 1662.

†Alexander Schmemann, *For the Life of the World: Sacraments and Orthodoxy* (Crestwood, NY: St. Vladimir's Seminary Press, 2004), 79.

PART TWO

Rest

For thus said the Lord GOD, the Holy One of Israel,
"In returning and **rest** you shall be saved;
In quietness and in trust shall be your strength."

Isaiah 30:15 ESV

We, Who Are Weary

I borrowed a Book of Common Prayer from a church a few years ago, and never had the heart to return that beat-up old red book. I don't advocate stealing prayer books. But as I cracked it open day after day and prayed through its pages, the prayers inside that worn little hardback with matching cloth tape on the broken corners became such an important part of my everyday life that I couldn't bear to think of life without them. And I couldn't replace that humble, broken, thumbed-through book with a crisp new one that only I had loved. I needed the fingerprints of other saints and sinners on the pages, encouraging me to press on. Holding that book in my hands was holding on to grace.

One of my very favorite prayers from that BCP is from the Compline service.* It reads like this:

Be present, O merciful God, and protect us through the silent hours of this night, so that we, who are wearied by the changes and chances of this fleeting world, may repose upon thy eternal changelessness; through Jesus Christ our Lord. Amen.†

Every day life pulls me in so many directions that I feel wearied by the changes and chances of this fleeting world.

My husband, my daughters, my friends, and the people I pass in the street all need me to talk, to feed, to help, and to serve in a hundred different ways at the same time. Plus, the ground under our feet doesn't feel stable these days. Every time I go to the store, one of the products I use daily has new packaging or it is discontinued, relocated, or changed in some way. I end up standing there in the grocery aisles, befuddled and trying to figure out how I'm going to wash my hair, brush my teeth, or eat breakfast in the morning.

The way we feel overwhelmed on a daily basis—born out of such small things but feeling like death by a hundred thousand paper cuts—tells us something about the times we live in. The world moves fast right now: Communication is instant and all-consuming, workloads are constantly demanding, and no matter who you are, financial security is not so secure anymore. So many of us feel small and completely insignificant in this whirlwind of change and chance. We think of our personal worth only in terms of how we can contribute something positive to the world. We grow weary and despair that there is anything we can do. The idea that we could stop and rest on God's eternal changelessness comes as a complete (and sometimes appalling) surprise.

Rest goes against everything we think we must do to succeed and find salvation in this world. We have forgotten that there is nothing we can *do* to find salvation. We cannot save the world. We cannot even save our own souls or the souls of those we love. That is not our business.

Our worth is not in what we accomplish. It is not in how much we sacrifice ourselves for the cause. It is not in how much we can give. It is not in how many people we can help. Our worth comes from the fact that God made us, God breathed us into life, and God loves us. Weary and all.

Our business is to do our daily work well, and then to rest. To carve out spaces for rest in our lives where we can set aside time to just be—not *do*, but just be—until all of our life rests on God.

———

*This word is often pronounced "Com-plin," which rhymes with "long pin." It is a little set of prayers handy to say in the fifteen minutes before crawling between the blankets of your bed at night.

†The General Synod of the Anglican Church of Canada, "An Order for Compline," Book of Common Prayer Canada (Toronto: Anglican Book Centre, 1962), 727.

Go for a walk

Lace up your shoes, grab a drink of water, and go for a walk.
Preferably outside. You might not have to go out of your way
to do it. Park a little farther away from work. Take the stairs.
Pile the kids in a stroller and get out the door. Don't think of
it as rigorous exercise. This walk is not about goals to achieve
or mile markers to hit. Enjoy the feeling of your feet on the
solid ground, your swinging limbs, and the air rushing by. For
a few minutes, just walk.

Walking will teach you what professor Loren Wilkinson
said in a class I took years ago at Regent College: "Our bodies are more than just a convenient way to carry our heads
around." We are more than a brain on a stick. He was teaching us about the dangers of mixing into our Christianity the
heresy of Gnosticism—the belief that our physical bodies are
evil while our spiritual souls are the only thing worth caring
for. A few days later, I learned on a walk how very important
it is to give attention to my body in the world.

After some all too heady work in the library, I was walking
home to my apartment on campus by what I liked to call the
"scenic" route. Instead of walking through the bus loop with
its field of gray cement and polluted air, I turned toward the
tree-shaded sidewalk across the street that ducks behind a
hedge and onto a quiet residential street. Not two steps in
that direction though, my sandal caught on a huge crack in

the sidewalk. For a moment of panic, I felt suspended in the air, then I fell down hard (with all the extra mass of a backpack full of books) on my left knee, putting a hole in my new jeans, my knee, and my pride. As I sat on the ground and saw the damage, tears sprang to my eyes. I was stunned and my knee was throbbing. I felt about three years old, completely stripped of the other twenty-plus years of a clean record of walking. I limped home feeling genuinely hurt but also feeling silly at how easily I was leveled. No matter how much education I have or how many years of walking experience, I am still susceptible to gravity and to a childlike reaction to my own pain.

This moment of remembering (painfully!) that I'm a person in a body also reminded me of the earthy Biblical imagery of stumbling. A lot of talk in the Bible is about people falling down who had it coming to them. Like Proverbs 26:27, for example: "Whoever digs a pit [to catch someone else] will fall into it." But what I learned from my own unexpected physical tumble was that spiritual stumbling can also come as a surprise.

I can be a pretty nasty perfectionist. My first thought when I fell was self-blame: "What was I thinking?!" But in a quiet place in my heart, God reminded me that of course I didn't do it on purpose. I had fallen without warning.

As hard as we try, we can't keep ourselves from falling by our own vigilance. Eugene Peterson writes about the hazards of modern pilgrimage: "We take precautions by learning safety rules, fastening our seat belts and taking out insurance policies. But we cannot guarantee security."* Instead, it is more helpful to practice the prayer from Psalm 69, which Abba Isaac, one of the Desert Fathers, recommended to John Cassian—"Come to my help, O God; Lord, hurry to my rescue"[†]—so that when we find ourselves on the ground sore among the leaves and dirt, our first thought is not blame but humility. For Teresa of Avila writes that there is no one in the journey of humility who is "so much a giant that he has no need to return often to the stage of an infant and a suckling."[‡] But by the grace of God, we all fall like little children and skin our knees. And by the grace of God, we can get up and try again.

Walking can create a space and time to attend to God. I've recently started strapping my youngest into her stroller (after we drop off her sister at preschool) and going for a walk around our local reservoir. The exercise is good for me, but I walk to remind myself of my body in the reality of God's created world. As I lift my feet and set them down again, they become a basic rhythm to focus my wandering thoughts. I move in the creation. The wind stings my eyes and they water. I smell the sharp brown scent of a freshwater lake. I squint in the brightness of the morning. A few dry leaves rattle on the trees or across the road. I lift my feet and set them down again, and I think about the basic miracle of ground beneath my feet. I think of how it is that I live and move and have my being in Christ. That God's love is good soil I can sink roots into like the trees around me have put their roots into the ground by the water. The grace of God is evident all around me.

On a walk, I realize anew with gratefulness and relief that it is God's world I live in. I am not the center of that world. Reality doesn't depend on my big head full of coherent thoughts. René Descartes had it all wrong when he said, "I think, therefore I am." It is not because I think that I exist— that would be to deny the wholeness of *this* real experience in *this* world. God is. God created this world and created me out of the dust of the earth and the stars. Therefore I am here today walking.

I don't need wealth or riches to walk. I don't need money for a car or a bike or a train ticket. I don't need fancy athletic clothes or even shoes in many places. I don't need ideal weather. I don't need sidewalks or a perfect neighborhood. Walking helps me remember to be grateful for what I do have: a good body (healthy or unhealthy), solid ground, safety, community.

I close my eyes, feel the sun, wind, rain, or cold on my face and pray: *Thank you, thank you, thank you.*

———

*Eugene Peterson, *A Long Obedience in the Same Direction: Discipleship in an Instant Society* (Downer's Grove, IL: InterVarsity Press, 2000), 38.

†John Cassian, *Conferences* (Mahwah, NJ: Paulist Press, 1985), Conference 10, 132–35.

‡Teresa of Avila, *The Book of Her Life: The Collected Works of St. Teresa of Avila*, Vol. I. Trans. Kieran Kavanaugh and Otilio Rodriguez (Washington, DC: Institute of Carmelite Studies Publications, 1987), 129–30.

Write down what your five senses experience

Find a piece of paper and a pen or pencil and write down what your five senses have experienced in the past twelve or twenty-four hours. I first discovered this practice on my friend Cindy's blog years ago. In blog posts titled "five-sense Friday," Cindy wrote down what she saw, heard, tasted, touched, and smelled throughout everyday normal Fridays. She didn't write every week, but when she did, it often stuck with me. I found myself thinking about the everyday things she recorded long after I read her post, seeing meaning and beauty in the trees casting shadows on the sidewalk, the winter sunlight slanting in the blinds and landing milky gold on a white wall, the warm, slippery bathwater, or a steaming cup of hot tea. I decided to try my hand at recording my own "five-sense Friday" posts. Since I'm not very good at doing things on time, and since I like to feel unique and spice things up a bit, I would often see her post on a Saturday and decide to capture my own "Sensuous Sabbath" in a blog post.

The task was simple, but powerful. For a few minutes, usually toward the end of a day, but sometimes earlier, Cindy and I sat down at our computers to think about what we had physically experienced that day. What did we see? What did we hear? What did we taste? What did we touch? What did we smell? We were trying to notice our days, to attend to the small things that we had encountered that day. Sometimes it took several minutes' reflection for me to remember: What *did* I eat for breakfast this morning? What *have* I touched? Often I'm so focused on accomplishing tasks that I'm just not giving my full attention to my physical presence in the real world around me.

These lists turned noticing everyday life into a kind of poetry. They were full of ordinary things like smelly cloth diapers, piles of books, computer keyboards, soft baby skin, poppy seed bagels with cream cheese, cold coffee, and hot tea. The lists helped us sift through the intensity of wild days that felt like sensory overload. They revealed glory in the daily miracles we encountered week after week, month after month. Food, shelter, touch, pleasure, disgust, longing.

More than anything else, writing down what had happened in a day made me slow down and take note that I had so very much to be grateful for. Sure, those diapers were stinky to begin with, but I also got to smell them fresh out of the dryer after the miracle of hot water and soap and blown air had transformed them. Sure, it was a little annoying to wake up at 5 a.m. to a rousing rendition of "Twinkle, Twinkle, Little Star" sung in a tiny voice, but it was also beyond beautiful. Even the simplest foods have so many amazing smells and tastes!

The colors in my life became brighter, the tastes became richer, the textures more welcoming, the sounds clearer, the smells more concrete and memorable. I always ended a list feeling as if I had met God.

That might sound odd to you. Met God? Isn't God beyond what we can see, touch, taste, hear, and smell? Is the whole physical world God? How can God be in the tree shadows, the winter sunlight, and the slippery bathwater?

Our physical experiences are a visible, tangible means of God's invisible, intangible grace. Our presence in the world is a present, a lowercase *s* sacrament. In my church tradition, we have two uppercase *S* Sacraments—Baptism and Communion. These are physical actions we take as a church to wash one another in water and eat and drink together in order to live out God's grace. But God's grace isn't limited to church. We can live it out in every other place on earth too. Lowercase *s* sacraments remind me that "in Christ all things hold together" (Colossians 1:17) and "in Christ we live and move and have our being" (Acts 17:28). Jesus Christ is the reality that holds every atom and molecule of the Universe together every day. Likewise, everything in this world exists because God chooses it joyfully and with complete abandon every instant of every day.

God is less like us, the weary, and more like a small child full of wonder and tireless energy. When a child sees something she enjoys, she asks her favorite adult to "do it again" over and over until that beloved person falls down from exhaustion. It is possible that our God, who brought the world into being, who sustains it daily by love, "is strong enough to exult in monotony," as Christian writer G. K. Chesterton puts it. Chesterton goes on to say, "It is possible that God says every morning, 'Do it again!' to the sun; and every evening, 'Do it again' to the moon. It may not be automatic necessity that makes all daisies alike; it may be that God makes every daisy separately, but has never got tired of making them.... The repetition in Nature may not be a mere recurrence; it may be a theatrical *encore*."* The everyday rhythms and routines of creation are likely held in place by a God who finds a rush of joy in them every single time.

Make your own list. Start by writing out, "Today I'm... seeing...hearing...tasting...touching...smelling..." and giving yourself the space to fill in what you remember. Take note of what God has done. With the wonder of a child, look into God's eyes to exclaim, "Encore! *Do it again!*"

---

*G. K. Chesterton, *Orthodoxy* (Garden City, NY: Image Books, 1959), 60.

Play with a child

Not long ago, when I was weary from parenting two little girls and wanted advice about how to enjoy my everyday life a little more, I came across an article on a parenting blog by Dr. Laura Markham. In it she suggested something I had not thought of, a simple activity I had never imagined. She said to set a timer for ten minutes and give yourself permission to spend the time in focused one-on-one play with one of your children each day. Let the child choose what they would like to do, but also include a few minutes of roughhousing play to help the child release the stress that accumulates naturally through the *big* emotions they deal with in everyday situations. She claimed that just ten minutes of focused time on a regular basis would help the child feel secure and accepted and improve your relationship all day long. Growing up, my mother called this "filling up a child's love tank." But the child is not the only one who benefits. Spending time with a child reminds us to take a little time to play.

Spend ten minutes with a child. Try to practice attention in all its physicality: turning your face toward the child, inclining your ear, opening up your heart. These are all the ways that our Maker cares for us, like a father who attends to his children. Try them out.

First, you will have to find a child. For those of us who are parents, that will not be hard (though finding a good time in your daily schedule to allow one-on-one time might be harder). For those of us who are not parents, it will take a little more effort and planning. It might involve calling up a friend or family member with a child, and saying, "I'm reading a book about connecting with God, and one of the assignments is to spend ten minutes playing with a child," then inviting the family over, asking to spend a few minutes after an event, or finding a time to meet up at the playground.

It's possible the family will be flabbergasted by your request. We tend to hang out with people who are like us. If we don't have kids, it can feel strange to be around kids. If we do have kids, we can sometimes feel like a traveling circus, a chaotic mess on wheels, or a natural disaster that leaves nothing but destruction and mayhem in our wake. So an invitation to spend time together might be startling to both of us. But make the invitation. Singles and families in different stages really do have so much to offer one another, not in spite of but *because* of our differences. Once the family gets over their surprise, they will likely feel relieved, blessed even. For ten whole minutes they will have one less child to worry about. For free!

When I was young, single, and childless, a mother and father of five in our church invited me over to their home for Sunday lunch on a regular basis. I wasn't awesome at playing with their kids, but their kids were awesome at playing with me, loving me, and inviting me to try new things. I often arrived feeling stiff and awkward and left feeling relaxed and joyful. As I left their house one day, I turned back at the door-way and thanked this mother, and she said the most amazing thing to me: "I feel so selfish keeping all their love to myself all week. I'm glad to share it! They just love being with you."

Those children had not yet lost the ability to enjoy time spent just being together with other humans. Once their basic needs are met, they, like most children, had the ability to let go and *play*. When we spend time with a child, we rediscover the ability to see the world with wonder and imagination, to look past things as they are and see the beauty and story hidden in plain sight.

You could spend your ten minutes with a child:

- **Running around.** Children have so much energy to expend. It's hard as the weary adult to imagine having this much energy ever again, but if you get up and get moving, you will most likely be amazed by how invigorating it can feel. Play Ring Around the Rosie or Duck-Duck-Goose. You will likely end up on the ground laughing.
- **Observing the world around you.** Go for a little walk around the room, around the yard, or around the neighborhood. Point and explain. Watch for wonder.
- **Doing magic tricks.** Where did your nose go? How did a coin get behind that ear? Is this your card? They will probably make you work for it, but watch for that huge, round-eyed, soul-stretching "Wow!"
- **Reading or telling stories.** Dig out a favorite children's picture book and share it with the child. Try retelling a favorite fable or fairy tale. Or if you are feeling especially brave, make up a story. Maybe one about a

brave princess who passes as a knight to kill a fearsome dragon, or a dashing prince who must give up his kingdom to save someone he loves. I know, I know we don't have princesses and princes anymore. All the better, your story requires *imagination*, that most neglected of virtues.

Whatever you and the child want to do, take these ten minutes to rest in God. The world will go on without you while you learn from this little person how to live beyond necessity again with wonder and imagination. For such is the Kingdom of Heaven.

Rest and the Fear of the Lord

I often come into God's presence with the wrong ideas about work and rest. As I prance into the throne room, I think I can make myself look good to God. I think God wants only perfect people in the room, and smiling, I say, "Look at me! Look at me! Look at all I've done for you! Lord, surely I deserve a little space at your right hand!"

Then, if I take the time to look around, I can clearly see that God's throne room is full of the lame, the blind, fishermen, beggars, outcast women, and outsider tax men. I find it hard to be around them; I don't know where to look or what to *do*. What I'm busy looking away from and avoiding is the fact that I am not so different from these people, only better at pretending. People come here to fall at God's feet because they know they don't have much of anything to offer to anybody, let alone God. They come when the grind of life has worn away their sense that the world can't go on without them. They come when they have nothing more to lose.

There is so much I am terrified of losing. So much comes between me and falling on my knees to speak the tax collector's cry, "God, have mercy on me, a sinner!" To rest in God and find my security in God means letting go of my tidy, beautiful image, getting grubby fingerprints on my gleaming white walls, sabotaging my promising career, raiding my savings accounts and my retirement funds, turning away from the possessions and entertainments I've earned by the sweat of my brow, and handing over the unique cultural freedom that allows me to live from day to day without feeling tied down.

But I have *staked my identity* on these fleeting markers of worldly success. I come to Jesus like the rich young man who asked, "What do I do to be saved?" but I am *shocked* and *appalled* to discover that to rest on God's eternal changelessness means to let go of exactly who I have fought to become. God wants none of my striving, control, and ingenuity. God demands that I hand over the idol of good old hard work I carved from wood, plated with silver and gold, and bowed before in hopes that by some miracle of positive thinking and brilliant foresight, my thoughtful, well-planned work could prevent evil, pain, and death. I hug it to my chest, frown, and stroke its face.

Resting on God's eternal changelessness demands that I have no other gods but the strange, ancient Yahweh, the God of gods, the Lord of lords, the King of kings, who sits on storm clouds like a throne, who holds the lightning bolt in one hand and directs the wind with the other, who knocks my idol to the ground, then smashes what I have built with my sweat and tears. This Sovereign Lord, the God who stands flanked by a huge army of ready angels, is the only one with power enough to defeat evil, pain, and death. To my horror, I am much smaller than I thought I was. My work, my judgments, and my possessions are dust and ashes in the wind. To look this God in the face, I learn a cold new fear in the pit of my stomach. *Fear of the Lord.* It is not, at first, any kind of relief.

Yet... exactly *this* powerful, perplexing God chooses rest and invites me to join in. This God celebrated with joy after six days of making the good world. This God invites me to leave the idol of work in the ashes and instead to choose rest. This almighty Ruler smiles and beckons to me to set aside my task list, my need to prove that I am indispensable, my belief that without my diligent work everything would grind to a halt, and to join the feast and the party. It is my choice. The Lord creates, the Lord destroys, the Lord defends what is good and just and right in the world. Will I stand aside? Am I willing to sit down at the table with stunned thanks, to taste, see, and say, "Blessed be the name of the Lord"?

Make yourself a snack

Celebrate the end of your day by making yourself a snack plate and having a ten-minute feast. Take just a moment to give thanks that by whatever miracle: you did it! You made it through another day!

This advice goes against pretty much all the sound scientific evidence that suggests you shouldn't eat within two hours of going to bed. You don't have to do it *every* night. But try it at least once.

How do you like to celebrate? I enjoy: a few slices of cheese with some crispy, salty, allergy-friendly crackers (because such are the limitations of my life) and a piece of fruit such as a fig, an apple, or a pear. Mmm. Or a bowl of yogurt with a handful of nuts and a drizzle of honey. Or some tortilla chips and salsa. I have also been known to scoop myself a bowl of ice cream and sprinkle it with *all the things*: chocolate chips, coconut flakes, nuts, jam, cake, whatever I can find. Tonight I thawed a slice of leftover chocolate stout birthday cake that I was saving for a day that needed to end on a happier note. The cake did not disappoint.

Maybe you don't even need a plate. Maybe all you need is a glass or a mug. Pour yourself a small glass of milk, wine, or seltzer water. Wrap your hands around a warm mug of herbal tea or decaf coffee. Give God a toast.

Find what will bring that happier note to the end of your

day. Put your feet up and savor it. No distractions, no screens, just you, your thoughts, and a little something yummy.

I learned this little practice of rest when I had children and realized that we were all better off if they went to bed early. My children bring joyful noise and action into my life, but by the end of the day—every day—I crave quiet. So does my husband. On my best days when my two girls are tucked into their beds each night right on time and on the worst days when the marathon of tucking in feels like walking through a wading pool full of molasses, I try to mark the blessed arrival of quiet.

There is usually work that needs to be done. There is that pile of laundry to fold, a mildewy-smelling load to switch from the washer to the dryer (phew, how long was it waiting there forgotten?). There is work: evening meetings to dash off to, e-mails, reading, thinking, planning. There is the endless circus of the Internet beckoning me toward infinite delight (and interaction with actual human persons over the age of four). But all of it can wait for just a few minutes.

Why? Is this just another dairy advertisement suggesting, "Indulge: you are worth it"? What does stopping to snack *accomplish*?

This little celebration on a snack plate or in a warm mug teaches us the difference between indulging and celebrating. We indulge in what we know is bad for us because we feel we have somehow earned the chance to cheat a little. We think, "Look how good I've been, I can be a little bad and it won't hurt." When we celebrate, though, we enjoy what is good in thankfulness precisely because we are unworthy, we have not earned it, because the goodness in this world is a free gift to us from God.

I have some food allergies, but thankfully, dairy is not one of them. For me, dairy is a gift from the God who owns the cattle on a thousand hills. Fresh fruit and nuts are gifts from the God who planted trees in the Garden. Human creativity is a gift we can use to take milk and make out of it cheese, yogurt, ice cream, and chocolate ganache icing.

If we keep in mind that every pleasure we experience is a gift, we aren't tempted to overdo it, because greediness disrespects the gift itself. The more naturally rich a food is, the more slowly I savor it, and the more aware and grateful I am for it, the less likely I am to abuse it because it is *satisfying*. It is enough.

Thomas Merton, a monk and spiritual writer, put it this way: "It is enough to *be*, in ordinary human mode, with one's hunger and sleep, one's cold and warmth, rising and going to bed. Putting on blankets and taking them off, making coffee and then drinking it. Defrosting the refrigerator, reading, meditating, working, praying, I live as my fathers have lived on this earth, until eventually I die. Amen."*

We have made it through another ordinary day. Things did not go as planned, but we were enough to meet the day's challenges, thanks be to God. God's grace was enough. As we celebrate by satisfying our ordinary hunger, we rest in the fact that enough is enough.

---

*Quoted in Ronald Rolheiser, *The Shattered Lantern: Rediscovering a Felt Presence of God* (New York: Crossroad Publishing, 2001), 43.

Reconnect with a friend

Invest ten minutes connecting with a good friend. This may mean sticking around at an event to look your friend in the face and listen carefully to hear what they've been up to. It could mean calling them up out of the blue just to chat for a few minutes. It'd be lovely if it turns into an hour-long conversation, but even if there really isn't time for that, ten minutes, five minutes, a thirty-second voice mail will be enough time to make a brief connection with a person who knows you and whom you care about.

Your friend will most likely feel refreshed and encouraged that you thought of him during your busy day. It feels good to be remembered. There's something special about talking to someone you have a past with. You share jokes and memories. You don't need to explain yourself as often. You don't have to worry about whether they'll still like you if you say something a little stupid (or even really stupid). Once you've known someone awhile, you've already been there and done that and stuck by one another through tough times and rough patches. You have been through a lot of life together, so even if you haven't spoken in a long time, there is a cozy, known quality to your conversations. You can pick up right where you left off. You remember one another.

When you really look at the word *remember*, when you break it down into its parts, re-member literally means to put pieces back together. Its synonym *recollect* has the same sense to it, gathering back together. In this way, remember is the opposite of dis-member, to take apart limb from limb. When God remembers Israel in the Old Testament, it preserves them and holds them together as a nation. By his relationship with them, he is able to pull together the scattered memories and shared experiences that make up the people. And even when the nation is scattered into exile, God holds them in his memory, just waiting to put them back together and breathe new life into them like the army in the prophet Ezekiel's Valley of Dry Bones (Ezekiel 24). God takes dusty old bones and puts them back in order, then clothes them with skin and armor and breathes life into them. And so with us. As time wears us down and eventually returns us to the dust we are made from, God will remember us, to restore and make us new again at the resurrection. One day God will breathe new life into the re-made lungs for all of us who turn our faces to wait for that breath.

Friends also put one another back together.

Recently I spent time with my friend Brandi, whom I used to see on a daily basis about fifteen years ago. When we were students together, we shared meals, talked about our favorite books and works of art, debated many different topics, and thought deeply about the way the world is and should be. But time, work, and further study eventually took us to opposite sides of the continent. While I spend time on social media online, Brandi does not, so we hadn't kept in touch about what was going on in our lives.

"Oh yes," I thought, "I remember this!" It was good to be

with someone whose mannerisms, expressions, gestures, and even voice felt familiar. Though the years have changed some aspects of our lives, in so many other ways Brandi was still just Brandi and I was still just me.

Being with Brandi—connecting, catching up, telling stories, laughing, eating, making new memories—not only helped me put two and two together again about who *she* is, why she's such a great person, and why I liked her in the first place, but it helped put *me* back together again in the midst of a period in my life when I felt like I was falling apart. My life as a mom and a writer was stressful. It demanded more of me than I thought I could give. I was weary and having a hard time holding myself together. Making new friends where I lived had been difficult, and I was constantly worried what people thought of me. But I didn't have to worry about that with Brandi. As we chatted, I could share honestly about my joys, pains, and worries. Brandi knew immediately that *of course* a new opportunity on my horizon was perfect for me; it fit with both who I used to be and who I am now. She had lots of practical, trustworthy advice to offer me. We were able to share both our joys and our struggles and really see each other.

"Why haven't I kept in better touch?" I kept thinking. "What else have I been wasting my time on? Why did I spend so many years in self-pity thinking that picking up the phone would just be an interruption to Brandi's busy life?"

In our fast-paced, mobile, global world, I bet there's someone out there who would be glad if you took a few minutes to remember them. Hearing their voice will bring a smile to your face and your soul will sigh, "Ahhh!" Think of one of those people and give him or her a call. She might not be able to talk. It might take several tries to get past his voice mail. You might have to root around to find her number again. But even if the conversation is awkward, it will be worth it.

The poet Gerard Manley Hopkins writes: "Christ plays in ten thousand places / lovely in limbs, lovely in eyes not his / to the Father through the features of men's faces." God images forth to us not in deaf, dumb, controllable Idols we make, but in living, breathing, maddening, free persons. To learn to attend to another person, to listen and hear, is to learn to attend to God. Neither attention is easy most days, but both are good.

Enjoy that goodness with a friend.

Spend ten minutes with an onion

Spend ten minutes with an ordinary yellow onion. You will need a sharp knife and a cutting board. And you might want to sit down for this one.

Episcopal priest and home chef Robert Farrar Capon included a whole chapter about hanging out with an onion in his cookbook *The Supper of the Lamb*. Only *he* argues that "to do it justice, you should arrange to have sixty minutes or so free."* We are going to make our best attempt to fit this practice into ten minutes. There will be no justice for our poor onions, but we will have made a start.

Sit down at a table with your onion, knife, and board.

Wait—we are not going to cut the onion yet. Don't start peeling it either. Don't touch it. Begin with a good, long *look* at the onion. What do you see? How precise are we being when we call it "yellow"? It has other colors, too, right? How many other colors could you name? What shape would you call it exactly? It's not quite round. What are those dry-looking furry things on the end? Where do onions come from any-way? The supermarket? The mind of God? Have you ever seen one grow? I don't think I have . . . well, except when I leave them in my cabinet too long and the green shoots burst out that pointy end. They must grow underground. But that's hard to imagine because they never have any dirt on them by the time they get to me. How do they manage that? Can *you* see any dirt on those little roots?

Touch your onion. What else do you notice? How does it feel in your hand? What if you squeeze it? Does it have a smell? What is that outer skin like? Peel a little off and look at it closely. Use your knife if you have to, but gently. It's surprisingly tough stuff. Brittle, but stingy. Try to take off as much as you can and leave it in a pile. That's the job I give my little girls to keep them busy when they are helping in the kitchen. It takes forever, but that's the point. Now you are beginning to get down a little closer to the heart of this onion; you are getting to know each other.

Cut into your onion. Set the onion up on its roots and cut down from the tip to the root. The layers are so amazing, aren't they? It's also kind of amazing how so much milky liquid the thing was holding. And whew! That smell! This is the part where my kids go running away from the smell and that burning feeling. It'll get a little better...One of my friends taught me a trick that onions kept in the refrigerator don't sting the eyes so much, another friend told me to keep a metal spoon in my mouth, but either way, you may need a tissue.

If you can get used to it, spend a few minutes looking at the layers. Peeling them apart, noticing the membranes and the innards. You can taste it if you are feeling brave. Get up close and personal with this living, growing thing. Get to know its glory and intricate detail. It's a little strange to say, but as our guide Robert Farrar Capon puts it, it seems like onions exist because "God *likes* onions, therefore they are. The fit, the colors, the smell, the tensions, the tastes, the textures, the lines, the shapes are a response...to his present delight—His intimate and immediate joy in all you have seen, and in the thousand other wonders you do not even suspect."*

You see how we could spend an hour at this?

An activity like this that invites us to give our full attention to something that we normally spend little time with teaches us an important lesson about what we were really made for. "Man's real work," says Capon (excuse his gendered language, what he means is *a human's* real work), "is to look at the things of the world and to love them for what they are. That is, after all, what God does and man was not made in God's image for nothing."* When we attend to the world, stretch our souls toward even the smallest things like onions, we are living out our purpose. And here we thought we were on earth for something much grander and more complicated.

Let this realization be your rest. God made you to notice and enjoy this good world. He made you not to fix it or improve it or maximize it, but just to marvel at it with love. Even a smelly yellow onion.

———

*Robert Farrar Capon, *The Supper of the Lamb: A Culinary Reflection* (New York: Smithmark, 1969), 11, 17, 19.

Pray a prayer already written down

We have come a little way from the foot of that sheer mountain face we started out looking at hopelessly. As we made our beds, planted our seeds (did they grow, by the way?), set our tables, washed our dishes, wrote our friends, confessed our sins, walked through daily life, and so on, each time we picked up one foot, stretched it forward, and set it down, to our surprise we are climbing.

We had the wrong idea at the foot of that cliff, and we've done our best to move past it. Prayer is not as much about us as we thought. Our effort, our offering, our sacrifice, our love. And yet it *is* about us approaching the throne of grace with all of ourselves: our anger, our blame, our shame, our pain, our love, our stuttering wonder. It is all grace. So we can take a deep breath.

We are trying to keep pace with Jesus, our Guide along this mountain path. His pace is strange and sometimes so confusing. We want to keep powering ahead. But Baron Friedrich Von Hügel has a word picture for us:

Experienced mountaineers have a quiet, regular, short step—on the level it looks petty; but then this step they keep up, on and on as they ascend, whilst the inexperienced townsman hurries along, and soon has to stop, dead beat with the climb....Such an expert mountaineer when the thick mists come, halts and camps out under some slight cover brought with him, quietly smoking his pipe, and moving on only when the mist has cleared away....You want to grow in virtue, to serve God, to love Christ? Well you will grow in and attain to these things if you will make them a slow and sure, an utterly real, a mountain step-plod and ascent, willing to have to camp for weeks or months in spiritual desolation, darkness, and emptiness at different stages in your march and growth. All demand for constant light, for ever the best—the best to your own feeling, all attempt at eliminating or minimizing the cross and trial, is so much soft folly and puerile trifling."*

Relationship with God is a long, slow journey up a steep mountain. We can't control the conditions. We must conserve our energies. We must use what tools we have wisely. And we must be willing to wait.

In order to do all this, we have to remember that, as spiritual theologian James Houston puts it, "The focus of prayer is not prayer, but God himself."† No number of tools that teach us "how to pray" are ultimately going to work if we lose sight of God's face. We are not climbing this mountain to reach the summit; we are climbing to be with God along the journey.

Take another deep breath. This can be intense. I've spent years fearfully avoiding prayer because I wasn't quite sure I wanted this much closeness. Could I trust this powerful God to walk with me? Was God good? Would God ask of me things I didn't feel able or willing to do? Ultimately—though we don't want to hear it—the answer to these questions has been "yes." Yet there was Jesus with his slow plod on the path as I exhausted myself running ahead. He has been a good Guide. Walking with him has bent my definition of "goodness" back into its proper shape.

If we are willing to end up a little bent back into shape, how do we go forward? How do we make conversation with God? Listen? Slowly get to know our Creator?

Try praying a prayer already written down for you.

There are strengths and weaknesses to this approach—sometimes it is hard to get your heart behind other people's words or words so often repeated you've forgotten what they meant—but ultimately it is solid. Written prayers give you a chance to rest in God's presence, to hear from the Word, and to learn from the wisdom of others. You are not so busy thinking up what to say next to sound clever, witty, or wise. Written prayers are a great relief on the days when you find yourself blank with nothing at all to say.

The best place to start is praying from the Psalms. I like the Anglican Book of Common Prayer in its many different forms, editions, and translations, but be aware that it steals all its best lines from the Psalms. For example:

O Lord, open our lips, and our mouth shall show forth thy praise.‡ (Psalms 51:15)
O God, make speed to save us, O Lord make haste to help us.‡ (Psalms 70:1)

Christians have found praying and singing the Psalms a good way to turn our faces toward Christ since the very beginning of our faith. The Psalms often give us the words to say things that we otherwise can't express. They help us deal with our emotions. They lead us in all our messes to God.

Thomas Merton brings this out in his book *Praying the Psalms*. Even when Psalms begin in a place that is uncomfortable for us—full of anger, war, frustration, abandonment—they end in a place of peace with God:

> No matter whether we understand a Psalm at first or not, we should take it up with this end in view: to make use of it as a prayer that will enable us to surrender ourselves to God.... We simply need to take possession of these Psalms, move in to them, so to speak. Or rather we move them into the house of our own soul so that we think of our ordinary experiences in their light and with their words.[§]

Pull up a facing chair for Jesus. Hold the words of your Psalm or prayer book in your lap. Speak each line aloud, feel the spirit-breath God has given to you on your lips. Pray through whatever fleeting thoughts come to mind, and hold them out to Christ. Listen in silence.

Let someone else's words help you surrender your ordinary self to God. Let that be enough.

---

*Baron Freidrich von Hügel, *Selected Letters 1896–1924*. Ed. Bernard Holland (New York: E. P. Dutton, 1933), 305, 226.

[†]James Houston, *The Transforming Power of Prayer: Deepening Your Friendship with God* (Colorado Springs, CO: NavPress, 1996), 44.

[‡]The General Synod of the Anglican Church of Canada, "An Order for Morning Prayer," Book of Common Prayer Canada (Toronto: Anglican Book Centre, 1962), 6.

[§]Thomas Merton, *Praying the Psalms* (Collegeville, MN: Liturgical Press, 1956), 26–27.

Enough Is Enough

We can't survive without rest. Our addiction to busy activity has given us "a weary that rest can't reach," as Abraham Lincoln put it to a friend. We are thinking of rest as an exclusive destination like an expensive fantasy vacation we can earn by working hard enough. Ronald Rolheiser says, "We imagine [rest] as a peaceful quiet place; us walking by a lake, watching a peaceful sunset, smoking a pipe in a rocker by the fireplace. But even in these images we make restfulness yet another activity, something we do, something we are refreshed by...and then return to a normal life from."*

In contrast, Rolheiser describes restfulness that will give relief as "a form of awareness, a way of being in life. It is being in ordinary life with a sense of ease, gratitude, appreciation, peace and prayer. We are restful," he says, "when ordinary life is enough."*

It is a rich thing to bring the restfulness of time away into the habits and routines of everyday life. What makes even the most daily activity restful is when we look back toward God with the genuine wonder of thankfulness, the way a child looks to someone who has given her a gift she did not expect. Let your daily life be enough: your walking, your play, your prayer, your small celebrations, your friendships, your observations, your listening to others, and your attentive listening for God. Amen.

———

*Ronald Rolheiser, *The Shattered Lantern: Rediscovering a Felt Presence of God* (New York: Crossroad Publishing, 2001), 42–43.

Listen to someone else
read the Bible for you

If you have spent any amount of time as a Christian, you know how hard it is to read the Bible by yourself for daily personal devotions. Guilt, shame, frustration, and confusion build up over time and make this kind of reading harder and harder. Give yourself the space then to listen to someone else read the Bible for you.

The Bible was always meant to be read and understood in community. The original authors and their scribes and copyists who scratched these words onto scrolls made of papyrus would have been amazed and dumbfounded by the idea that in the future every member of the church would read these Scriptures by themselves every day. Not that they would consider it a bad idea once they wrapped their minds around it; they just never would have imagined what is an ordinary reality for us—we can all read and we all have our own Bibles, in many different versions, translations, and formats.

The ancient Hebrew and Greek believers lived in a very different world, where only a small class of people had access to education and literature, where writing was time-consuming and expensive, and where books were rare and costly. The church approached Scripture in community. They read, interpreted, pondered, and lived out the scrolls of ancient

Scripture, one book at a time, in community. In temples, in synagogues, in family homes (which also included servants, apprentices, and several generations of extended family), and in churches.

The idea that *anyone* can read the Bible is a victory of the imagination. During the Protestant Reformation, people *died* to get the Bible translated and printed into our daily language. In the centuries that followed, people worked tirelessly and thanklessly to teach reading and writing to those who weren't deemed "worthy" in the premodern world. Many of us would have fallen into that category, including about 99 percent of women and 90 percent of men. We would not have had any access to books or much of any ability to read. It is *a wonder* that you and I can read today.

But this miracle has come with a few potential pitfalls. Today, holding that Bible in our own hands without much of an understanding how it got there, we can fall prey to the idea that we can understand the Bible as we read alone. We can fall into the trap of thinking that whatever is immediately evident to us, reading alone at our desks, is the clear meaning of any given Biblical text.

Growing up, I thought that daily Bible reading and private Bible study were *the only way* to know God personally. But the more I tried it, the more I found it was like trying to sit on a stool with only one leg. It was possible to know God that way, but it sure was an awful lot of work. After a while I simply gave up, but giving up that one way to God felt like giving up everything. I still believed that to love God meant to take the Bible seriously. I had listened to its stories, memorized whole chapters, found my way around its books as if they were rooms in my own home. "Where is this?" someone would ask, and I knew exactly where it was.

The Bible was where I met God. At night when I couldn't sleep, God was in the pages of the Psalms. God was present to me in the stories of Abraham and Sarah, who longed for a promised son; of David the shepherd-king; of Jesus the God-man; of Paul the missionary. So many words in the Bible had been God's direct words to me—"Come unto me"; "Take up your cross"; "Go, sell all you have and give the money to the poor." But the more I read alone, the harder I fought to understand, the longer I studied, the less sense I could make of any of it. The farther and farther away God seemed to get.

I tried to meet God in personal devotions, and I failed.

So I let go. And I wondered if that meant I was letting go of God.

I wandered around for a little bit, wondering. I read a lot of books and articles about the Bible. I even tried to read the Bible without expecting God to be there, just to try to see it again differently. Some of this helped and some of it didn't.

Finally, when I was about to give up, I found a church where church members read the Bible aloud weekly. Then the minister explained the reading thoughtfully in a sermon that didn't teach from only one verse or jazz around topically, but *entered into* one book or passage of Scripture at a time, sometimes for a week, a month, or a year.

It was a tremendous relief.

Listening, I encountered the Bible a whole different way, in community with other Christians. We read the Scriptures aloud, each with our different voices, accents, emphases, pauses, and perspectives. I could follow along, volunteer to read, or just listen. What sank in, sank in, and what stuck out, stuck out. The whole weight of knowing God did not rest on my diligence for independent reading. I was able to see God more clearly in the passages when I read them and discussed them with others and focused the other six days of the week on living that out, not cramming in more.

I gave up my striving, and God replaced it with rest.

Find a friend or family member, in person, on the phone, or maybe even in church. Listen to her read a bit of the Bible aloud to you. Sit. Incline your head, stretch out your ear to the sound of the words. Chat about the passage for a moment. Carry around in your heart a phrase that sticks out. Let it be enough to listen for the God who is present with you both exactly where you are.

Read a spiritual classic before bed

Take a few minutes right before you lay your head back onto your pillow to sleep and read a spiritual classic. James Houston defines the great classics of the Christian faith this way: "Books become 'classics' when they speak about the deeply felt, abiding principles of life before God, recognized across many generations among God's people."* These are books written by Christian believers to share personal experience with God that have guided many others to experience God.

My first experience with reading a classic of Christian spirituality was as a young girl—I must have been about fourteen. It did not go well. My Bible teacher at the Christian school I attended offered to give us extra credit if we read Augustine's *Confessions*. I found a paperback copy of it on my mom's bookshelf at home and cracked it open. I did not last long. I found the book confusing, and I felt stupid because I couldn't understand such an important book. Looking back now, I can see I struggled because *Confessions* was originally written in Latin in the fourth century, and the translation in that particular old paperback used old-fashioned language and did not flow well. Not all translations are so hard to read and understand.

But even as I struggled, I found *Confessions* intriguing. Augustine writes the whole thing as a direct conversation with God, as though he is telling God his life story and discovering its meaning through the conversation. He weaves in words from Scriptures as though they were his own words. And the way he takes the story of an everyday thing and shows how we can meet God in the tiniest of moments—like stealing pears with a gang of kids, hearing a sermon, reading the Bible in a garden, or spending time with a loved one looking out from a window—is breathtaking.

Ultimately, Augustine is drastically different than me. As a man from North Africa who lived 1,600 years ago during Roman rule, his life has almost nothing in common with mine. And yet, I was surprised to find out that though culture and politics have changed and though language and the rituals of daily life have changed, the foundational truth of what it is to relate with God has not changed.

We read Augustine because he is different than us. His perspectives challenge our preconceived notions about what it looks like to believe in God and have a relationship with God, ideas we have built up over time based on our experiences in the time and place where we live and the predominant culture that surrounds us. And we also read Augustine because he is the same as us. He struggled with some of the same things we struggle with as we search for God. He, too, battled with the reality that "our hearts are restless until we rest in [God]."† He puts into words what we know to be true and yet have no words for. He also challenges us because he takes God much more seriously than we do.* This kills a perfectionist like me who likes to compare herself to others and come out on top. And yet he motivates me to seek a deeper relationship with God.

Another Christian whose classic book has startled me into a better relationship with God is Julian of Norwich. Julian is also not like me. Julian lived in Medieval England, and in 1383, when she was thirty years old, she nearly died. On her deathbed, as she looked to a crucifix for comfort, she had an intense vision that the crucifix had come to life with blood running down it and Christ dying before her eyes. And then she had a series of conversations with God. Julian thought she was going crazy, but what she couldn't explain was that as she looked at the cross, she was healed. After her recovery, she committed the rest of her life to meditating on and writing down these visions for the benefit of others as an anchoress in one tiny room *with no door out* (only small windows) at a church in Norwich, England.

Although it seemed I had nothing in common with this woman, once I got past the strange Middle English of her writings, I was struck by how honestly and openly she talked to God. She asked God her hardest questions point blank. And they were my questions, too. Why do we sin? Why does pain exist? Why did Christ have to die for my sins? Why would he? And what is God really like? Spending time with Julian over the past fifteen years has given me the strength to believe in God at several points when I was ready to give up. Julian and I both desired to know God, and how we related to God was strikingly similar (even if I haven't had any deathbed visions).

There are many other fellow pilgrims on the path to relationship with God whom we can learn from: Bernard of Clairvaux; Teresa of Avila; John of the Cross; John Bunyan and his *Pilgrim's Progress*; Fyodor Dostoyevsky and his *Brothers Karamazov*; poets such as John Donne, T. S. Eliot, and Mary Oliver; and contemporary novelists such as Wendell Berry and Marilynne Robinson. The list could go on and on. Each of these writers shows us that though we may be from different cultures and languages and denominations, as Christians we all strive for the same thing—deeper relationship with God.

It is a tough sell to recommend these books to you, because they are not easy reading. But give them a try. Choose one, and give it five, ten minutes before bed. Set your timer and put down the book after your time is up. Try it again tomorrow, if you can swing it, or next week. Far from failing, you will get much more out of the books if you take them in these very small chunks. I've been working on Dostoyevsky in fits and starts for over two years, but I'm only starting to see the story now. This is not a homework assignment or an obligation; it is a chance to meet a new friend and mentor who can help you along the road. It is an affirmation: You are not the first down this path and you do not walk alone.

———

*James Houston, *The Transforming Power of Prayer: Deepening Your Friendship with God* (Colorado Springs, CO: NavPress, 1996), 47–48.

†Augustine, *Confessions*.

Take a day off

Part Two, "Rest," has thus far offered nine ways we can attend a few minutes at a time. This tenth one invites you to make a bigger investment in the project of rest, or to at least sit at rest and *imagine* investing more. Consider spending one whole day at rest. In the Bible, this practice was called keeping the Sabbath.

Small investments of time release us from the impression that relationship with God is only for the super-spiritual. Relationship with God does not happen only when we have hours to set aside for church or Bible reading or prayer. Relationship with God builds up through the small moments of our everyday lives.

But there is one problem with our small projects. In his book *The Sacred Year*, Michael Yankoski describes how something important happens when we practice rest for a whole day: We discover that when God made the world, our Creator did not initially set aside a holy place, like a temple, but a holy *day*, a holy space in time. Michael found this idea in a book by Abraham Heschel, and Michael and his wife, Danae, live out the idea weekly. When they practice keeping the Sabbath, Michael and Danae set aside one day a week to enter into God's holy space in time. They put their watches, cell phones, and even their wallets into a special box, and they live a day without obligations. Michael says, "It is a day for delight.

For sleeping in. For making love. For eating delicious meals and leaving the dishes until tomorrow. For taking long walks. For sitting in front of the wood fire and reading a novel. No chores. No obligations. No homework. No e-mail. No bills. Nothing at all that feels like work, nothing that seems to be oriented toward productivity or achievement."* He describes what this looks like for them one morning when they have a pancake breakfast with good friends visiting from out of town: "With no wristwatches to truncate the meal, the conversation ranges and flows, spreading out luxuriously. One hour? Two? Who's counting? We sit and we feast and we talk as long as feels right."*

The problem with setting our timers to five or ten minutes for daily connection with God is that our infinite, three-personed God cannot be contained in ten minutes. Of course, God cannot be contained in a whole day either, no matter how holy it is, but if we accept our Creator's invitation to set aside a whole day, it is a start. We can begin to live in a different relationship to time than the press we typically feel to be here by this time and there by that time and this person gets so much time and that person only a little bit more, and there is always so little time for ourselves. For six days there is never enough time, but on the seventh day (whichever day of the week you might be able to let that be), you rest. You choose to believe that life itself is enough.

The kind of rest that Michael describes, "feasting, delighting, and embracing," allows us to be really present in time to one another, to ourselves, and to God. This kind of rest is so different than the entertainment we typically fill our weekends with when we come exhausted to the end of a heavy workweek. Ronald Rolheiser says, "Because we are so busy what happens is that when we do have leisure, we can only spend it doing something mindless and distracting. There is no energy for anything else."[†] I find myself drawn into the mindless and distracting week after week.

But what if we could carve out a space in our lives for not just mindless, distracting entertainment, but re-creation? What if there were a way to be with God without having to set a timer to keep us on schedule? Can you imagine that?

Though some of the grind in my life as a mother to two young children never goes away, our family does keep a Sabbath. For us that means setting aside one day when we don't work. No chores. No billable hours. No writing for projects, e-mailing, or telecommuting. No obligations. Our family is all together and we try to do something life-giving that can't fit into regular work days. We go to a new park, visit a hiking trail, have a picnic lunch, or play a game. On a particularly rough week, we let one another sleep in shifts until we feel halfway human again. We chose the Sabbath through periods when my husband, Clint, had three jobs and was in school full-time, through newborn stages, and through big transitions. I'm pretty sure it's the only way we survived the toughest times with our lives, minds, work, and marriage intact.

Try it. Take a day off. Plan ahead so you can sleep, spend time with loved ones, and live into God's holy time.

I do want to warn you, though. After you've had a good sleep, a nice breakfast, and a few minutes of gratefulness, you might start to feel a little off. One doctor who treated many Christian and Jewish patients for "the sudden onset of headaches, stomachaches, and attacks of depression they experienced every Sunday" called this "Sunday neurosis."[‡] Sometimes the Sabbath has a darkness to it. It draws attention to needs in your own soul that you have pushed aside in your busyness. It makes space for boredom and beneath that boredom may be tears, anger, frustration, pain, memories, or grief.

If the Sabbath is a space to just be, you may as well just be yourself. No masks. No hiding. Give attention to your own soul. What have you been carrying around like a ball and chain, just trying to ignore? Is there a way to be free of it? Enough is enough. You don't have to live that way.

Choose God's rest instead. Let go of more, of excess, of baggage. Be satisfied. Let God be God. Let rest be enough.

---

*Michael Yankoski, *The Sacred Year* (Grand Rapids, MI: Zondervan, 2014).

†Ronald Rolheiser, *The Shattered Lantern: Rediscovering a Felt Presence of God* (New York: Crossroad Publishing, 2001), 41.

‡Barbara Brown Taylor, *An Altar in the World* (New York: HarperOne, 2009), 136.

PART THREE

Quietness

For thus said the Lord G od, the Holy One of Israel,
"In returning and rest you shall be saved;
In **quietness** and in trust shall be your strength."

Isaiah 30:15 esv

Listening to Silence

A few years ago, I saw a remarkable film called *Into Great Silence*. The movie records six months at a Carthusian monastery high in the French Alps where the monks observe a vow of silence. They live their lives, for the most part, without speaking. Six days a week they live in their own individual cells, coming out only twice a day for sung worship in the chapel. Then once a week, on Sunday, they spend time together and have a chance to talk.

Before I saw this film, I had a certain idea about what life observing a vow of silence would be like. A life of total silence appeals to me. For the most part, I am a sensitive, quiet person in a big, noisy life. I long for someone to just turn the volume all the way down to nothing. I want peace and quiet on my own terms, unbothered and not distracted by anything. I thought the monk's life of silence would be— well, it's so obvious as to be ridiculous—absent of noise. The thought that someone could capture or watch a film about this kind of life seemed strange.

What *Into Great Silence* revealed was that I had no idea what monastic silence was about. Plunged into a world without talk or background music, I felt more aware of every sound. Every drip of water. Every footfall on a stone floor or a snowy path. Every swish of a pair of shears cutting fabric.

Every buzz of the clippers on the appointed day for haircuts. Every resonant prayer chanted by candlelight in a night-dark chapel. It was beautiful, but it was also deeply challenging.

The monks' lives were not lives of absolute silence as an escape from the noisy world. Though in one way their lives were quieter, in another even the smallest of actions became an almost unbearable, unavoidable cacophony. Those men did not find in the monastery that by closing their own mouths, they could quiet the whole world. Those monks' lives—at their best—became lives spent straining to listen. Spending time with them, even in a limited way through the film, I found they were good teachers. It dawned on me that I was not listening to my own life very closely.

Watch the sunrise or sunset

It's surprising these days, in our indoor lives, to remember that the sun still rises and sets every single day. I don't often stop long enough to witness the sunrise. I make lots of excuses why I can't. "I would watch more sunrises if they weren't so early in the morning," I say with a laugh. I would watch more sunsets if they didn't fall at the busiest time of day, the cooking-dinner-bedtime routine marathon. Or on the daily commute when my eyes are on the road, not the horizon, and I'm more concerned about putting down my visor to shade my eyes than looking into the brightness. The sunset just makes a frustrating commute more unbearable.

We like to forget that the sun rises every morning and sets every night because it irritates us, the same way our daily self-care, food preparation, and housekeeping chores irritate us. "The sun rises and the sun sets, and hurries back to the place where it rises," cries the Teacher in Ecclesiastes (1:5 NIV). "Meaningless, meaningless...utterly meaningless! Everything is meaningless" (1:2 NIV). One day's work is done then by the next day it has come undone. Just in time for us to do it all over again. We are so small on this spinning earth.

We are powerless to make the sun rise or set. Nothing we do can make the days long enough to pack everything in, or short enough to catch our breath under the pressing weight of uncertainty, misery, and grief.

"The sun rises and the sun sets and hurries back to the place where it rises."

But there is a second way to see the sun rise and set, if we are willing.

We can watch in quietness. Open the blinds at the breakfast table. Take the dog for a well-timed walk for a few minutes after dinner. Pause for just a few minutes. Suspend judgment just long enough to watch and wonder.

No two sunrises or sunsets are ever the same. They do not happen at the quite same time two days in a row. They do not happen in the same place in spring or summer as they do in fall or winter. The sky is filled with clouds that catch the light in ripples and shadows, or the sky is clear and alive only with an uninterrupted gradation of color and light. The light catches on a lake or under a thunderstorm, and the whole world is transformed by reflected color that permeates the very air.

We do nothing to deserve the miracle of yet another fresh new day, or the relief of another night's rest for our tired bodies. The sun rises, a new day's possibility. The sun sets, a new night's relief. The promise is new every morning and every evening; God has not yet given up on us. "Encore!" God calls joyfully to the creation. "Do it again!"

The sun rises and the sun sets, and *with a great rush of joy*, it hurries back to where it rises. Like a little child bouncing in the wings at a school play, who asks over and over again, "Is it my turn yet? Is it my turn?" Then the director says, "Go!" and glory breaks onto the stage.

When we sit in quiet long enough to watch a beautiful

sunrise or sunset, we learn a gentler version of the fear-of-the-Lord we glimpsed as we learned rest in the presence of Yahweh, who sits on the clouds. Eugene Peterson describes this beautifully: "The moment we find ourselves unexpectedly in the presence of the sacred, our first response is to stop in silence. We do nothing. We say nothing. We fear to trespass inadvertently; we are afraid of saying something inappropriate. Plunged into mystery, we become still, we fall silent, all our senses alert. This is fear-of-the-Lord."* Again, we find this mystery of encounter with God in our everyday routine. But we have reset our perspective, ever so slightly, to give credit where credit is due.

Look up what time the sun will rise or set where you are and set yourself in the way of God's everyday grace. Watch for it on a walk, through a window, with someone else, or alone. Pull your car over; play in the backyard with your kids; sit in silence as the rays slant orange on the wall of your hospital room. Be still and know that God is God. Our Lord is not giving up on us.

———

*Eugene Peterson, *Christ Plays in Ten Thousand Places: A Conversation in Spiritual Theology* (Grand Rapids, MI: William B. Eerdmans, 2005), 41.

Take a deep breath

Find a comfortable chair or a position on the floor where you can sit with your back straight, your heart lifted ever so slightly to give your lungs the space they need, shoulders pushed down and back, your arms and legs at rest, your palms open to the heavens. In the quiet or the noise, in the brightness or the dark, feel the breath that comes into you and out of you. Try different kinds of breaths, short quick ones and long deep ones that fill your lungs all the way to the bottom. Set a timer if it will free you to focus.

Not long ago this description would have made me feel uncomfortable. Sitting around breathing seemed to have more to do with Eastern mysticism—yoga, Buddhist meditation, mindfulness—than it did with Christian faith. These practices seemed self-centered and body-centered, and they had nothing in common with the rational, doctrine-focused Christianity I knew. I was under the impression that our bodies and their desires were bad, to be trained, subdued, and resisted. I was deeply disconnected from my body and confused about what it meant to breathe every day. But the Bible kept challenging these assumptions in ways I didn't expect. I started digging deeper in the Scriptures, looking at images, metaphors, and root words. Suddenly, the whole book lit up like a pinball machine.

Ruah. Pneuma. Spirit. The ancient words (in both the

Old Testament and the New) for "spirit" also mean "breath" or "wind." The very first word picture we have of the three-personed God in the Bible is a Wind hovering over the face of the deep, rippling the water with a loving Breath, dreaming joyfully how to make that formlessness into something good (Genesis 1:1–2). Then, after a week of preparations, Creator God bends down close to the earth, the Word forms a person from the clay with a proud smile and a sideways glance—"Isn't he just like us?" (Genesis 1:27)—and the Holy Wind puts breath into that first earthling's mouth and nose, filling lungs and turning an Image formed of the dust of earth into a spirited living being (Genesis 2:7). Splitting one so there were two (Genesis 2:22). Feeling the heat of the blame they breathed out (Genesis 3:12–13). Filling the lungs of their baby as he cried his first breath (Genesis 4:1). Meting out justice to the brother who stilled that first son's breath when his blood cried out (Genesis 4:10). The blood and the breath belonged always to the Giver of Life.

God came to this earth in a tiny, gasping baby body, sucking in and pushing out our air 80,000 times per day just like any of us did as newborns, gradually slowing down until the day God heaved out one last Breath of grace and forgiveness in the face of a terrible death. But who could still that breathing for good? How could a death-sigh be Life's last breath? Our God breathed again into the body stilled by violence and hatred and the chest lying still on a slab in a tomb rose and fell once more.

And when the time was right, God did not leave us alone. That Holy Wind stoked fire in God's people and pushed breath into a new Body, the Church (Acts 2:1–4). That Holy Breath gives us life, such an undeserved gift, day after day, until at last it slides out and returns to God. And one day, nearly beyond our imagination, God's Wind will gather the dry broken pieces of us, re-member us and breathe new life into those put-back-together, made-new bodies, so that we can be in the presence of our Light and our Breath and our Reality forever.

Those of us tempted to believe that our Creator and King shortchanged us when Jesus left us only a wispy, nebulous Ghost-self, will benefit from spending ten minutes with the startling gift of our breath. The life we take for granted every day is the gift of God. God is present with us every few seconds. When we sit down and when we stand up. When we go to the right or the left. When we make grave mistakes and when we live in the bold realities of God's Kingdom.

Our breath can be our prayer. We breathe in the oxygen of grace—"Jesus Christ, Son of God"—we breathe out the carbon dioxide fumes of sin and weakness—"have mercy on me, a sinner." We catch that startling grace in our lungs to breathe it out to others.

Inspired, our breaths drawn in, our bodies filled with Spirit, our spirit-baptized imaginations run fast, loose, and free. We hear a voice behind us calling, "This is the way, walk in it" (Isaiah 30:21). And what a good little way it is. Our God goes before us leveling mountains and making the path straight (Isaiah 40:4). We run in the path of God's commands, for love has set our hearts free. We run, heads thrown back, arms loose in the air, straight down a path leveled for us by grace beyond imagination, outlined by God-breathed Words (2 Timothy 2:15) we thought we knew but we now know with our whole aching selves. And the more we run, the more our lungs long for new breaths.

Stop and catch your breath. Breathe. Pray. God is as near to you as this very next breath.

Light a candle

Light a candle, and let that little dancing flame light the face of God in your life.

Find a candle. Find a match. Strike that match. See the little flame. Hear its tiny sizzle and whoosh. Smell the sulfur burning on the tip. Now you are in a little race. Before the heat pinches your fingers, get the wick of your candle lit. Watch the flame grow bigger, then split as you pull away the matchstick and blow it out.

A candle burns on the table in front of me as I write. I bend near it, smell its rich fragrance. The flame stands still and straight in the quiet of this afternoon. Time slows down a little as I watch the little pool of melted wax at the base of the flame grow larger. Heat rises in little waves that blur the wall behind them slightly. I hear the wall clock ticking. Little hopping sparrows chatter outside the window.

Lighting my candle gives a special sense of intention. It is time to focus. This is time offered up to God. For writing. For prayer. Just to be here, sit here, do my good work here. As the room fills up with the candle's unique scent, I feel more present. I don't have anything else but here and now, this quiet room on a hazy afternoon. So I offer up what I have. This moment. Here and now.

We don't really need candles to light our lives like my

grandparents did in their earliest years, but I'm glad we still keep candles around. Ironically, I learned the spiritual power of lighting a candle online, from writer Sarah Bessey. When a tragedy makes the world cold and dark, Sarah often lights a candle, and her little flame flickers across the world and through my screen to give me peace.* Lighting a candle helps us give our full attention. At a meal, turning out the brighter lights in favor of softer candlelight brings us closer together. The world around the table we share fades from view. With distractions hidden in shadow, we can take a deep breath and focus our attention on the sparkling eyes across from us. The low light creates a space for more personal conversation, for a richer sense of the smell and taste of the dinner. Cut glass and silver shine with glory. On an evening alone, the gentle flicker of candlelight gives a sense of peacefulness and rest to time spent in a bath or with a book. Candles on a birthday cake burn more brightly every year with the glory and mystery of life.

Candles on the table at a Jewish seder supper, on the altar at a Christian communion service, or among the people gathered on a holiday like Christmas Eve seem to invite and represent God's presence among us—the Creator-King sits down with us to eat, the dusty Savior offers himself on the altar of sacrifice in our place, the Wise one lights our way through the darkest places in life one step at a time. The candles remind us that each human face made in God's Image shines with a glory beyond what we see in the brightness of day.

To keep a candle burning requires our attention. Candles shouldn't be left unattended. There is a little warning in the back of our minds as we move about a room where a candle is lit, as we watch to make sure that we don't reach across it and set loose sleeve, long hair, or nearby paper on fire. We watch the flame to make sure that the drafty air or an overeager toddler won't blow it out before its time. We watch to trim the wick when it flares up too wildly. Like priests keeping the lamps in the tabernacle, we tend that little candle and let its light remind us of our prayers and our commitment to God's presence with us.

As you light your candle and allow it to burn, set aside some time to notice God's presence with you in the quiet. Stretch toward God with a specific request. Your candle is a little offering, a little vow to give your full attention. Offer up a news story burning a hole in your heart. A friend in labor to bear a child or up all night with a newborn. A relationship that is broken. A surgery under way. An illness that is claiming the precious life of a friend. A worry or care that invades the quiet of your life. Let the flame lift up your prayer as it flickers and dances, melts and burns, gives off its heat, smoke, and fragrance. One small, fiery dot of brightness against the darkness and pain of the world.

God longs for us to burn with love, too, to be little lights against the darkness of the world, to tend our wicks so that they are always ready for the flame of presence. God longs for us to let the Spirit burn brightly in our hearts, purifying us and throwing light on the road ahead. To burn but not be consumed. God longs for us to tend the flame of love for

God and others, which will burn out if we do not choose to watch it carefully.

Light a candle and sit with God. See what the light and the darkness have to show you.

———

*Sarah Bessey, *Out of Sorts: Making Peace with an Evolving Faith* (New York: Howard Books, 2015), 145–46.

The Strength of Quietness

Earth's crammed with heaven
And every common bush afire with God;
But only he who sees takes off his shoes,
The rest sit round it and pluck blackberries.
　　　　　—Elizabeth Barrett Browning, *Aurora Leigh*

You and I are not monks living under a vow of silence like the monks at Grande Chartreuse. We do not live in the quiet of a monastery. We have taken no vows of long, enduring silence. Our lives are noisy: full of tedious, good work, family relationships and friendships, plugged-in communities, and daily pleasures. We would likely find a monastery a very uncomfortable place. Our ears would ring with all that creepy silence, a sudden ability to hear every drip of water would drive us mad, and the clattering sounds cooking in the kitchens of our own souls would quickly become torture.

Learning to live in quiet is a little bit like the odd old story about the prophet Elijah meeting God at Mount Horeb.

World-weary from his work as a prophet, Elijah waited in a cave for God, who had told him to wait there. A great wind whipped up, "splitting mountains and breaking rocks in pieces" (1 Kings 19:11 NRSV). But that was not God. An earthquake shook the ground. But that was not God. Then there was a fire. But that was not God either. Finally, after the fire, there was, as the New Revised Standard Version translates it, "a sound of sheer silence" (v. 12). A footnote in the English Standard Version calls it "a sound, a thin silence," and the main text translates it "the sound of a low whisper." In The Message, it is "a gentle and quiet whisper." In the King James Version, a "still small voice." Every single version of the Bible seems to come up with something different!

Apparently, to the best of our guesses, the sound of God's arrival was something like a deep, resonant silence, or perhaps a sound so small, complete silence was necessary to hear it. This whisper-silence brought Elijah out of the cave to listen as God gave him a new assignment. In quiet connection with God face-to-face, Elijah met with the strength and purpose to go on.

Learning to live in the quiet presence of God, to bite the tongue, and to rebuke the inner restlessness of the heart takes time to adjust and it also takes a certain strength of character. It forms in us a strength we never knew we could have.

Spend ten minutes in God's creation

Spend ten minutes surrounded by living, growing things in God's creation.

I used to live a short drive away from the deep, green fir and spruce forests of Pacific Spirit Park on the University of British Columbia campus in Vancouver, Canada. On quiet days when Clint and I could carve out a few minutes, we would head over there, park our car along the shoulder of a busy four-lane city road, and head off into the trees.

The well-kept trail, recently built up with soft mulch, was springy under my feet. As the path forked and I moved deeper in among the trees, a quiet descended on the old-growth forest. The trees filtered out the noise of the cars on the road we'd left behind. I could smell the black earth, the red wood, and the sharp, green needles. Even on a hot summer day, the temperature dropped several degrees as we pressed farther into the forest. The air felt cool and damp on my face. The light was shadowy and green as it filtered through the canopy of the massive Douglas firs, towering between one hundred and two hundred feet above my head.

When we walked in the forest, I was always surprised by how much calmer I felt. Tension melted out of my shoulders. My breathing and heartbeat slowed, despite the light exercise. My eyes adjusted to the lower light, feasted on the rich natural colors. I paused to wonder at huge slugs crossing the path, leaving a shimmering thread of slime behind them. I shivered past spiders hanging in their webs in a beam of sunlight. I gawked at lilies growing in marshy ground, listened to birdsongs, walked, watched, and listened closely.

It was years later that I learned that attention deficit disorder specialists recommend time in creation as an ADD therapy, even something as simple as looking at a tree outside your window or having a green plant in your home. It is good for attention to spend time among green created things. When I wander in Vancouver along forest trails or stony beaches, in Southwest Oklahoma through yellow prairie grasses, around low, sprawling green cacti, and over worn, red boulders, or even across the leafy green woods and grassy meadows of Central Park in New York City, the world that I work so hard to maximize and prioritize and optimize melts away. I can let go of my illusions of grandeur. I can let go of the pressure to control, and feel the tension melt from my muscles. In creation, I enter a world where my primary business is not to control, but to notice, with wonder, so many small, beautiful, infinitely complex things I did not make and I cannot manage.

It feels obvious to say that you and I have no power to create a world out of nothing. Of course we don't. We are only human.

So why do we keep trying? Why is my imagination bent toward constantly attempting to create small worlds I can control? Why is it that my default position is to assume I am at least a small *g* god?

We live in a world of pure rationality on our computers

so much of the day, where it feels as though we *can* create physical worlds out of so very little—ones and zeros, codes, images, and words. We live in a world where advertising bombards us daily, sometimes *thousands* of times a day, with the message that we can create our own happiness, and don't *you* deserve to be perfect and beautiful and happy? What is a perfect life according to the world we live in today? Well, it is one that is controlled, balanced, neatly trimmed, perfectly coiffed, well behaved. A perfect life is the fruit of our toil, the shining image that we create by the sweat of our brows: posed tranquillity, smartly dressed children, homes always ready for a magazine photo shoot, manicured feet on the ground in the world. Chaos or beauty beyond belief could be just outside the frame of the photo, but all we focus on is the image.

I haven't found it very rewarding trying to be a god. I'm worn out. But how do I fix my broken imagination?

Stretch the muscle of your attention and let out the tension of controlling life, by spending ten minutes attending to something that only God could create. This little stretch is a scaled-down version of a task described in *Scattered* by medical doctor and ADD sufferer Gabor Mate, a concentration exercise one of his patients, Andrea, learned from a Native American elder. Andrea says, "She told me to sit in a meadow, measure out with my eyes a patch of ground one yard square, and do nothing but gaze at it for an hour. I got to know every blade of grass, noted the different textures of fallen leaves, followed every movement of ants and ladybugs, and the time went before I knew it. I was never so exhilarated. I have done it many times since."*

None of us are immune from the effects of attention deficit disorder these days, especially the spiritual ADD that attacks our souls and distracts our attention toward many false satisfactions. Find one square yard to attend to. Set your timer for two, five, ten minutes. If sitting makes you stir-crazy, find a path and walk down it. Take the time to see, hear, taste, touch, and smell the world around you, a world full of beauty and complexity, unity and harmony, growth and peace. Full of danger, chaos, decomposition, and mess. Notice the colors, the textures, the patterns, the fragility. You may be surprised what you find.

———

*Gabor Mate, *Scattered: How Attention Deficit Disorder Originates and What You Can Do About It* (New York: Plume, 2000), 253.

Make something with your hands

Stretch your soul toward God by making something with your hands. As you make, pray. There are as many different ways to try this as there are people. In a way, this type of unceasing prayer bleeds over into every quiet good deed in this book. Here find something repetitive, mindless, and time-consuming, and use the quiet of that activity as a space for prayer. This could be working on a handicraft: knitting, whittling, crochet, coloring in a coloring book, refinishing wood, scrapbooking, painting a wall, cross-stitching, making a piece of furniture, hand lettering, building a model car or airplane, or quilting. Or it could be something else entirely: building a sand castle, playing with clay, mowing grass, driving, swimming, jogging, or boating. What is important is that your hands or your body are engaged and attentive but your mind is a little free.

Holding something in my hands focuses my thoughts. And my thoughts often need focusing. On a typical day, my thoughts bounce around from family responsibilities to writing ideas to theological problems to ways to fix the beloved tiny plastic thing one of my children just broke. Everything gets all jumbled up and I can't tell which thing is important, which other thing is important but doesn't have to be done *right now*, and which thing isn't important at all. So I worry.

I'm good at worrying. Worry is like a gossipy old friend whom I cringe to see again but quickly fall into conversation with.

So last year I taught myself to knit because I had some free time on my hands and I wanted to quiet the worry.

When I knit, all I have to think about is the next stitch. Do I put my needle in front to back and loop the new yarn from the back, or do I put my needle in back to front and loop the yarn from the front? How many of each kind of stitch do I need? How do they fit with the row I just completed and the row yet to come? All these questions keep my brain busy enough to forget my worries. It is not still exactly, but it is quiet. As I get used to these stitches and their patterns, they become routine. And in the quiet, I can pray.

After my first knitting project, a small scarf, I decided to go big and make a simple prayer shawl. At least twenty years ago, a women's prayer group was looking for a meaningful practice of prayer and created a group of prayers and a pattern for knitting a shawl out of stitch patterns of three—for the three persons of God. The practice caught on and spread and now includes knitters all over the world making beautiful, useful things out of their prayers. I checked out the *The Prayer Shawl Companion* from the library, and carefully selected which shawl I would like to try. As I thought about whom I would like to make the shawl for, at first I thought I would like to give one to a friend who was grieving or going through a difficult time. But I realized how much I needed to make something not to heal or encourage someone else, but for my own soul. I chose a gray yarn, since gray can symbolize wisdom, and a basket-weave stitch, to remind me how I am not alone, but woven together with so many other Christians in Christ.

As I knit, I lit a candle to set apart the time. I prayed one word for each stitch. *Jesus, Jesus, Jesus. Loved, loved, loved. Grace, grace, grace. Father, Son, Spirit.* Those gentle, true words stitched together into a tiny fabric on the needles. My stitch pattern repeated six stitches in a row so I fit it to the Jesus prayer. *Jesus Christ, Son of God,* have *mercy* on *me.* (It sort of worked.)

The words of the prayer measured my stitches, and my prayer slowly came together into a growing fabric. Rather than my usual prayers that seem to pass over my lips and fall straight to the ground, or if they get some air, they just gather in the corner of the ceiling like a bunch of helium balloons, this prayer was one I could see, touch, remember, keep close to me, and eventually wear buttoned and wrapped around my body. One long thread of yarn, one long prayer, woven through days and months into something I could keep to remember how I met God as I knit that shawl.

Making a shawl, a table, a model, a castle with your hands in repetitive motion creates a space for quiet in your life. You will find that quiet space is almost never neutral. One day you enter it and hear only the grim voices of self-doubt and self-hatred growing louder and louder as you cling to your prayer like a lifeline. Another day you come and feel the prayer fill your soul like wind fills the sail on a sailboat, pressing you forward through the breaking waves toward love. At the end, your work stands as a physical evidence of that battle in the quiet, physical evidence that in both the terrible times and the good times, God is here.

Yes, God is here. Invisible grace is present in the physical things we see, hear, taste, touch, smell, and make here and now, in the next few minutes. This is not an airy-fairy mystical mystery, or even just a metaphor; this is the solid ground of our faith. God gives us the raw materials of this world: sheep's wool, cotton plants, and plastics, as well as the creativity to spin, knit, sew, and transform their raw, messy natural beauty into orderly, beautiful, and useful offerings. In love, God gives us these gifts to cover our nakedness, to give us warmth from the often cold existence of life in the world, to heal raw, painful places in us. We accept the gift and give thanks, by putting our hands to work.

Making something with our hands connects us to the reality of God's provision. This work is not a waste of good time that could be spent saving the world. You are saving the world here, one prayerful stitch, coloring stroke, whittling stroke, or glued panel at a time. You have come to the cave on Mount Horeb to meet God not in the wind, the fire, or the storm but in the mundane, the repetitive, and the everyday, in the silence of clicking needles and love.

Give a gift

Plan and give a gift to someone in your life who could use a little love.

Not a large or elaborate gift. It doesn't need to be expensive. You don't have to spend days or weeks planning. What you need to do is find a way to physically hand over a little evidence that you are paying attention.

Giving and receiving gifts can be painful to think about. For many of us, gift-giving brings to mind Christmas fails, disappointing birthdays, and times when our expectations were high but the people we gave to or received from just weren't attentive. We wore a thin smile and said, "Oh thanks, Grandma, socks!" But inside we felt unnoticed. Or we remember a time we agonized over what to give someone we love, but the gift missed the mark. The whole enterprise can become so painful and fraught, we no longer bother— instead, we pass out Amazon gift cards, or just declare that we have too much *stuff* already so we are not giving gifts this year and don't expect any in return. The physical items we give have no meaning beyond themselves, and we'd just rather not have them at all. We wonder in our shame and sadness: Why do we even give gifts in the first place?

I learned from my grandmother Frances Ketchum that the best physical gifts we give carry love into everyday life. Though she had twenty grandchildren and our family didn't live close by, I never got socks, so to speak, from Grandma Ketchum. She was very good at stretching toward us with her full attention. I was never once disappointed with a gift she gave me. In part, this was because Grandma had so many gifts to give that she made a gift-giving plan. For many of our birthdays, we knew we could expect a certain thing. When we turned five, she made a simple quilt in our favorite color. When we turned thirteen, she crocheted a colorful afghan. When we turned sixteen, we got a piece of silver jewelry or a watch that connected with our Norwegian heritage. In the other years, she bought things from our Christmas and birthday lists, and I knew that as long as I asked for something reasonable and on budget, I could count on finding that thing under the tree on Christmas morning or under wrapping paper on my birthday. I learned from Grandma that the most meaningful gifts build a quiet trust. The thing itself, spread on my bed or worn around my neck on a special day, helped me experience the dependableness of Grandma's love, even long after she died. Grandma created that security, by the work of her hands and her careful planning.

A gift is powerful when it is attentive. A gift makes us feel loved when it meets a need in our lives. When it is exactly what we wanted, even if we never realized that until we held it in our hands. When it is something we don't think to provide for ourselves, but should. A gift hits the mark when it is exactly what we long for but never imagine in our wildest dreams that we could have. A great gift-giver sees a need that we don't even see in ourselves. An amazing gift is not just more stuff, but a gift of the Giver's attention and care.

For one moment in life you knew that someone noticed you and cared for you. You knew you could count on their love.

My younger daughter gets gifts that surpass her imagination all the time. But much to my chagrin, they are almost never those big gifts that I buy her for a proper gift-giving occasion. Not quite two years old, she is consistently blown away by everyday gifts. "Wow! Yook at it, Mommy, yook at it!" she exclaims at the most surprising moments of everyday life. Look at the cows in that field! Have you *tried* that banana pudding? Look at the birds at the birdfeeder! Look at my sister! Look, there are *blueberries* on my plate! Just *look* at this whole big amazing world! To see the world through her eyes reminds me that life itself is an incredible gift.

Daily God gives us gifts of attention, presence, and peace. The word *grace*, which we use to describe our right relationship with God, meant in New Testament Greek simply "gift." Unlike other types of gifts in the ancient Greco-Roman world, gifts given to patrons in thankfulness for their support, gifts given with the expectation of something in return, God's gifts to us are given freely and lavishly, with no strings attached. The gift of another breath. The gift of a pumping heart. The gift of an intricately designed creation full of the evidence of our Creator's loving care. To show the full extent of love for us and the world, God took on a body like our own frail, aching bodies. God gave up power and position to become a tiny baby, a young child, an awkward teenager, a physical laborer, then a wandering rabbi. Jesus gave us the gift of God's physical presence on earth. Each of these gifts are visible signs of God's invisible grace.

We imitate God's surprising, attentive gifts by giving to one another. Because nothing we have truly belongs to us to hoard and keep anyway. Life, blood, breath, time, work, service—they all belong to God.

Give a small gift, a physical representation of your love and goodwill for someone. Silence inside yourself the static noise of "I can't do this," "I don't know so-and-so well enough," "I'm not good at gifts." Spend a few minutes quietly attending to someone you know or someone you love, just long enough to notice what they really need. This often takes less time than we think it will, when we listen in the quiet of our hearts. It might cost us time, effort, money, but give from what you have, no more, no less. Don't do it to get anything in return. Don't let your left hand know what your right hand is doing. The gift you give is your attention and your love.

Finding Quiet

The activities in this section aim toward two goals: external quiet and internal quietness. To seek external quiet, we turn off the noisy inputs in our lives: media, opportunities, responsibilities, even friendships. These are not bad things, they can be very good things, but they fill up the small silences in our lives to the point where we don't really know how to be quiet and alone anymore. So for a little while, we turn them off. This will create space that makes quiet possible.

Seeking inner quietness is where things really get hard, though. When we cut away the noise we use to fill our lives, suddenly we are left with ourselves. And it can be ugly. Our hearts make more ruckus than everything else in the world put together. Make space to listen to the din inside your soul. Then let our Mother-gentle God hush and quiet that precious soul, like a mother who hushes her weaned child, a child who no longer *needs* her but who basks in her love and attention (Psalm 131:3).

Inner quiet is harder to find than outer quiet, but it is more portable. You take your soul with you everywhere. If you can find quietness when you are alone before the face of God, you can bring that happy quiet into even the loudest, busiest places. Quietness becomes a state of being in all of life.

This quiet, wherever you can find it, is your own cave on Mount Horeb. Look our Holy God in the face. Strain to hear God's loving whisper in the solitude of the everyday wilderness. Let quietness give you strength to face your plain old everyday life.

Sit with someone in pain

Some people seem to find it easy to sit with someone in pain. I have to force myself to stay with people in pain, people who are ill, people who are broken. All I want to do is run. Other people's pain is messy and inconvenient. It reminds me of my own pain. And my pain reminds me of my own very concrete, physical limits.

When I see someone in pain, I just want to be able to fix it. I want to be able to make it go away. Being in the presence of someone else's pain becomes almost physically painful to me, taunting me with my powerlessness to help. My daughter's pain when she skins her knee. My dad's pain after a cancer treatment. How quickly I would act to take it all away!

It has taken me a long time to believe that pain could have any good purpose.

I have suffered my share of physical pain, enough at least to know how destructive pain can be. I suffer from fairly regular migraine headaches. At worst, a migraine can consume up to five days at a time.

For the first few days, I generally try to bear up under the pain and rest a little. I try to keep as close to my daily schedule as I can. But if the headache hasn't lifted by the end of the third day, I begin to despair that it will ever go away. I cry, I rest, I pound on my bed pillows. Resignation gathers and sustains me until I realize with surprise that the pain, my constant companion, has finally left. The whole world feels new again. My heart swells with gratitude for the beauty of the world. The light, the green, the gentle breeze. Who knew that it had ever been so beautiful?

Life is painful. Living in the modern world can feel like walking out into a hailstorm. We are assaulted on every side. Our skin stings with the pelting ice. We feel at constant risk that the hail could get too big, that it could snuff us out. But I learned from Peruvian poet César Vallejo that sometimes "so much hail falls so that I will remember and appreciate the pearls I have gathered from the mouth of every howling storm in life."*

Pain can make us grateful for the simplest things in everyday life like nothing else on this earth can. The pain of hunger drives us to eat. The pain of thirst forces us to drink. In the pain of cold, we seek out warmth. In the pain of heat, we draw back from what would destroy us. The pain of injury or infection causes us to stop, rest, seek treatment, and wait for healing. In my darkest pain has flashed out beauty that I never imagined could exist.

Pain teaches us that we are not God. That is the only justification for pain that God offered to Job in the Scriptures. "Were you *there?* Could *you* make a world? Then hold your tongue." We do not get the rest of the story.

But God was so committed to this very human story, including puzzling freedom, sin, and pain, that God put on skin to enter the story with us. In the person of Jesus, God became human to suffer with us, and when that was not enough, to suffer in our place the death we had freely chosen over and over again as we chose life apart from Life itself.

Time after time throughout the Scriptures, the first action that God takes when the people cry out in pain is to come and be with them. God hears the cries of Israel in slavery in Egypt. God hears the cries of injustice throughout the period of the Judges and the Kings. God hears the cries of Israel again in exile in Babylon and Assyria. God shows up again and again as Immanuel, God with us (Isaiah 7:14). This is why you should look attentively in your life for someone in pain and go to them. You are not God; you cannot take the pain away. But be like God; do not leave anyone alone in their pain.

You may not have a lot of time to invest today. But there is at least one person in your life who is in pain and crying out to be noticed and to be *not alone*, however briefly. Sit with a child who wails as though every tiny bump and bruise were the end of the world. Call an elderly relative far away. Send a note, a small gift, or a care package. Show up in a hospital room or a home to hold someone's hand or chat for a few minutes. Whatever you can do, do it.

It's okay if it's awkward, if you don't do that great a job of it, if you say the wrong thing. Err on the side of saying little. Be quiet, watch, listen. Ask a question, bring a board game, offer to do a specific chore. Just be there, set aside your "busy" to make space for a person broken open by his need. To stretch toward that person is to stretch toward God. When you take the time to be with her in her pain, you take the time to be with God.

One of my favorite writers, Glennon Doyle Melton, says boldly that sick time is her time to shine. When her children, or other people she loves, are sick or hurting, she knows just what to say. These are the words she uses to be with someone in pain:

"This is awful. I know it hurts—and I can't take it from you. But I'll stay right here and hold you until it's better."[†]

These words have a lot to teach me. They acknowledge the pain with compassion. They acknowledge our limits. And they stick to the one positive thing we can do: *Be there*. In body, in soul, in love.

———

*This is my own translation of the first lines of César Vallejo, *Trilce*, LXXVII (Madrid: Catedra, 2006).

[†]Glennon Doyle Melton, "Best New Year's Ever." Last modified January 1, 2016. http://momastery.com/blog/2016/01/01/best-new-years-ever/.

Pray with beads

Pray with a set of beads in your hands, to mark the physical progress of your prayers.

When I had been an Anglican for only a little while, I made a friend named Lucy, who gave me a Roman Catholic rosary one Sunday at church. She picked it up for me at St. Patrick's Cathedral in New York City. It had lovely iridescent blue beads and a big, sharp metal crucifix.

I was more than a little terrified by that string of beads. I was a good Evangelical Protestant Jesus-girl, even as my feet started on the road to Canterbury. I had grown up believing that the Roman Catholic Church got Christian belief wrong on some important points. Crucifixes, rosaries, and Hail Mary prayers were way outside my comfort zone.

Eventually, though, after years of keeping that rosary closed up in its little round case on my bookshelf, unsure quite what to do with it, I also discovered that there was such a thing as an Anglican rosary. It was simpler, with a plain cross, fewer beads, and more flexible, scriptural or historical sets of prayers. No crucifix. No prayers to Mary. But the same grounding practice of holding beads to count and focus my prayers. Holding the little circlet of beads while I repeated a set of prayers kept my anxious mind and fidgety hands busy and out of trouble. The beads arranged in four groups of seven meant it took about ten minutes to pray all the way around.

After trying in fits and starts to find the right prayers and set them to memory, I made my own little prayer routine out of a few prayers from Julian of Norwich that I had copied down and stuck on my bulletin board. Here is a little what that looks like:

Holding the Celtic cross on my beads, I pray:

In the name of the Father, and the Son, and the Holy Spirit. Amen.

Moving my fingers to the fat Invitatory bead above the cross, I pray a prayer from the prayer book (which, if you remember, stole these phrases from the Psalms):

O Lord, open our lips,
And our mouth shall show forth thy praise.
O God, make speed to save us,
O Lord, make haste to help us.

The first two lines of this prayer remind that it is God who gives breath and prayer. The second two lines call for God's help and presence. Early church theologian John Cassian points out that a person could live a rich spiritual life with God with only this prayer on her lips all day through every challenge and temptation of life.

Moving on to the large bead at the base of the circle of beads, I pray words from Julian of Norwich's first revelation:

We seek rest here in these things that are so small in which there is no rest;

> *And [we] do not know our God who is Almighty, all wise,*
>   *and all good;*
> *For he is true rest.**

Julian wrote these words in response to her vision of all of creation as small as a hazelnut in her hand (about the size of that big bead on my rosary). She saw that creation exists only by God's love, and that it is small compared to the Almighty God's great love for us. We will never find rest for our restless souls if we seek it only in the created things in this world. We must see those things as gifts of the glorious reality of relationship with God.

Julian prayed then, and I pray with her over and over again as my fingers pass over each of the small beads in sets of seven:

> *God of your goodness,*
> *Give me yourself,*
> *For you are enough for me.**

God is good. I need that reminder every day. God is not against me. God is not angry with me. God loves to give of Godself to satisfy me. One of Julian's most profound images from later in her book teaches me that Christ's self-sacrifice on the cross was a joyful sacrifice of love. Christ *chose* to suffer for my benefit. This prayer reminds me that God wants relationship with me, and I want relationship with God. God is enough for me.

Do I really live as though God is enough for me? I know *I* never feel like enough in this busy, weary-making world.

There is always something more asked of me. And not only that—I always need more. I eat and I am hungry again. I drink and I am thirsty again. But Julian's words call me back to reality. Give me yourself, God; you really *are* enough for me.

And so an Evangelical Jesus-girl repeats her prayers around an Anglican rosary borrowing the words of a Roman Catholic mystic who lived a very long time ago. On the large beads: *"We seek here rest..."* On the small beads: *"God of your goodness..."* When I have prayed all the way around and I am ready to close out my time of prayer by returning to that Invitatory bead, I finish with the Lord's Prayer:

> *Our Father in Heaven,*
> *Hallowed is your name,*
> *Your kingdom come,*
> *Your will be done,*
> *On earth as it is in Heaven,*
> *Give us today our daily bread,*
> *And forgive us our sins,*
> *As we forgive those who sin against us.*
> *Lead us not into temptation,*
> *But deliver us from evil.*
> *For the kingdom, the power, and the glory are yours,*
> *Now and forever. Amen.*[†]

And as a final word, gripping the cross, kissing the cross, and making the sign of the cross on my body by touching my forehead, my heart, and my two shoulders, I say the Glory:

*Glory be to the Father, and to the Son, and to the Holy
    Spirit,*
As it was in the beginning, is now,
and ever shall be, world without end. Amen.[‡]

Praying with beads might be a huge stretch for you. Or maybe you're dying to try this type of thing. If you don't have a set of beads on hand, you can make one with your own beads, or simply by putting knots in a string. Or you can follow along by printing out a picture and walking your fingers across the beads before deciding to take the plunge and buy one. Try my prayers or seek out others. Either way, give praying with beads a chance. Test out this gentle practice of prayer and see if it can silent the tumult of your heart and help *you* turn your face toward God.

————

*Julian of Norwich, *Revelations of Divine Love*. Ed. Barry Windeatt (Oxford: Oxford University Press, 2015), 45–46.

[†]The Archbishops' Council of the Church of England, *Common Worship: Services and Prayers for the Church of England* (2002–2004). Accessed via the Daily Prayer app for Android. Developed by Aimer.

[‡]I have included the traditional language here, though it uses male metaphors for God that make me uncomfortable when I really think about it. God is not male or female, but much bigger than our gender categories. Both male and female genders as well as all the complexity of life as a gendered human being reflects the Image of God. If you prefer to say a gender-neutral version of the Glory, you can say, "Glory be to the Creator, and to the Savior, and to the Holy Spirit…"

Make a to-do list for your day

Make a to-do list for your day ahead. Write down everything that is demanding to be done. Empty out your mind of all those worrying little things that should have been done yesterday, that absolutely have to be done by tomorrow, and that it would be hard to get through your day without getting done. E-mails to write! Bills to pay! Forms to sign for school! Paperwork to file! Chores to be done! Meals to eat! Whew. There is always so much gnawing at our minds to be done. Get it all down to quiet the nagging thoughts and the anxious worries that whisper to you all day that you are forgetting something.

Once you have that long(ish) list, tear the page off the top of the notepad or turn over a page in the notebook or open a new note in your favorite app and write down on your new list only the three to five things that need to be done today, in order of importance or in the order that you anticipate you will be able do them.

As you do these things throughout the day, mark them off your list by putting a straight line through them. This works a little more strongly than just putting a check mark by them. When you have a line through them, they are done, they are gone, the words no longer demand your attention anymore. Their whining voices are quieted. You can forget about them.

When you get to the end of the day, if you have any tasks left over, unaccomplished, try a little trick that I picked up from the book *Life Work* by the poet Donald Hall. Put a squiggly line through them. Quiet those unfinished tasks, too.

Here is why this is a wise thing to do. You might not want to completely forget about those tasks yet, but the world did not fall apart because you failed to do them. You can always try again tomorrow. But as you end your day, let it truly end, don't carry whispering voices of guilt or shame over to the next day. Don't write them on tomorrow's list yet. Tomorrow will have enough worries of its own. Let them go. If they are important, you will remember them when you have time to do something about them. You can still read them, mostly, on your sheet. You have them marked differently so that you can immediately remember that they were not yet done.

But at the end of the day, when the sun has set yet again, you have eaten and done the dishes and put children to sleep, you have had a cup of decaf coffee or herbal tea and chatted a moment with a spouse or a roommate or a family member near or far, you have done enough. What you accomplished that day was enough.

If you are afraid it was not enough, then you are not seeing clearly. Sit down for a moment and think about it. Write yourself a "Tada!" list to revel over all you *did* accomplish that day. You will probably surprise yourself. Look at your day. You did what you could. No one can ask any more of you than that. God doesn't ask any more of you than that. Sure, it is wonderful to learn how to maximize your workweek and make space for what really matters, but marking out the "didn't quite do" things on your to-do list is a great way to make that space. You have done what you could. Go rest.

Because the truth is that quiet and rest are connected. Rest, daily mandated rest and weekly Sabbath rest, is really important for achieving quietness in our souls. If we fail to rest, to put to rest our to-do lists at the end of the day, to revel with gratitude in the "Tada!" of all that we *did* accomplish by the grace of God, we will miss out on God's work. We will miss out seeing where God was at work in us in the ordinary things we did all day and where God was at work outside the margins of our carefully planned priorities. We can only see these things when we begin the day by limiting our to-dos to what one human can actually accomplish among the many tasks of keeping ourselves and those who depend on us alive, and when we end the day by quieting the noise of our own to-dos. Peterson is blunt on this point and he is right: "Without silence and stillness there is no spirituality, no God-attentive, God-responsive life."*

If you really want to know God, you need this type of quiet to remember that you are not superwoman or superman. You are just yourself. And that is more than enough. Rest those weary bones in thankfulness for the One who made them, and made them good.

———

*Eugene Peterson, *Christ Plays in Ten Thousand Places: A Conversation in Spiritual Theology* (Grand Rapids, MI: William B. Eerdmans, 2005), 118.

Spend ten minutes in quietness with God

This stretch toward God builds on and draws from the others we have done in this section. As we watched, breathed, lit, walked in creation, prayed, gave, sat, or repeated our prayers in the presence of God, those actions prepared us to sit with God our Friend in external and internal quiet. We have stretched and used the muscle of soul-quiet, until we know just a tiny bit what it feels like for God to quiet our souls within us. We did not strive out of self-control or self-discipline, but out of love and longing to know God.

Find a quiet place to sit, not in absolute silence, which you will never find, but in a posture of listening. As when you sat with your breath, sit comfortably, maybe in a chair with your back straight and feet resting on the floor or in a comfortable position on the floor. Do indeed sit. Nothing in your hands. Nothing to do. Nowhere to go. Just you—body, soul, spirit-breath, mind, heart (these are all saying the same thing, the wholeness of you)—the world around you, and God.

Pray with the Psalmist, "For God alone, O my soul, wait in silence" (Psalm 62:5). Turn away from the restless movement and busy noise of the world, and turn to God. James Houston describes well how stillness focuses us on God. "Becoming quiet before God means to reject all intrusions that might interrupt our being with God. Such intrusions could include noisiness, anxious thoughts, or even self-consciousness. This can be a hard lesson to learn. We can achieve stillness by having a simple approach to God—the approach of a child who simply trusts his parent."*

This *can* be a hard lesson to learn. You may feel like me. I *used to* trust God with this quiet, childlike confidence in God's love, some time ago when my faith in God and my experience of God's grace were brand new and exciting. I felt I could see God's goodness everywhere. But now I have been through a dry time, and I find it hard to trust like that anymore. Where was the Almighty, all-powerful God was when I went through pain, suffering, or rejection? This is a valid thing to ask God.

We can learn to move toward God again the way a trusting child moves toward her parent. Philosopher Paul Ricoeur calls this the "second naïveté." We have come through a period of critical distance, a reconsidering of everything we once assumed God to be like, and yet again God calls us close. If we come near in faith, it is now *by choice*.

God is the one perfect Parent. If we believe that, Houston says that the child's simple approach "allows us to enjoy God's acceptance, and to be filled with his assurance and his confidence. Prayer at this level happens when no words are expressed, no thoughts are declared, because God's presence surpasses all that our senses might declare. The thought of Psalm 46, 'Be still and know that I am God' is the climax of the life of prayer."*

Choose this simple approach. Choose to come near God with quietness and stillness.

Invite God's Spirit to be with you. Imagine Jesus sitting near you. As you sit, listen. As you hear an airplane roar overhead, a car pass by, a clock tick, or a voice speak nearby, listen. Give thanks. As you feel your breath come in and out of your body, your stomach rumble with hunger, yesterday's supper make its way through your intestines, or as you feel your pain, listen. Give thanks. As your thoughts rumble and rattle around your head, listen. Give thanks. As your soul cries out to God, listen. Give thanks.

Most likely, you will not have a life-transforming experience the first time you try this for any small set amount of time. It will feel uncomfortable, out of control. But sounds, feelings, sight, smells, become unhealthy distractions when we try to control them, silence them, shove them down. Because in many cases, we cannot. That is no failure in you. You have not failed to connect with God if you couldn't create absolute silence.

But let God's presence surpass all that your senses declare, as Houston said. Let yourself just be. Just be with God. No demands. No expectations. No agenda. God has no agenda for you at this moment. No, just be together. Just sit together. Just two, three, five, ten minutes, whatever you can offer.

When your time is up, breathe a word to close. Thank you. Amen. In the name of the Father, and the Son, and the Holy Spirit. Glory be to God. Lord have mercy. I love you, God. Find your own phrase. Whatever feels right. Take a few more deep breaths, let yourself come to the surface again.

Prayer is intense. It involves all of our being, all of who we are, exposed before God. It can be painfully hard to experience God's acceptance and love, especially when we have little or no love for ourselves. But God's love has the power to transform us.

Let quietness before God be your strength. Listen for God's still, small voice. Rest on your loving Parent like a little child rests on the one she loves best. Let this quiet confidence be your strength.

———

*James Houston, *The Transforming Power of Prayer: Deepening Your Friendship with God* (Colorado Springs, CO: NavPress, 1996), 48.

PART FOUR

Trust

For thus said the Lord GOD, the Holy One of Israel,
"In returning and rest you shall be saved;
In quietness and in **trust** shall be your strength."

Isaiah 30:15 ESV

But You Were Unwilling

I have not yet shared *all* of Isaiah 30:15. Here is the whole verse in its context (emphasis added):

> *For thus said the Lord GOD, the Holy One of Israel,*
> *"In returning and rest you shall be saved;*
> *In quietness and in trust shall be your strength,"*
> **But you were unwilling,** *and you said,*
> *"No! We will flee upon horses";*
> *Therefore you shall flee away;*
> *And, "We will ride upon swift steeds";*
> *Therefore your pursuers shall be swift.*
> *A thousand shall flee at the threat of one;*
> *At the threat of five you shall flee,*
> *Till you are left*
> *Like a flagstaff on the top of a mountain,*
> *Like a signal on a hill.*
> **Therefore the LORD waits to be gracious to you…**

In Isaiah 30:15, when Yahweh asks the people of Israel to trust, they are invited to find their refuge and their confidence in the God of Abraham, Isaac, and Jacob, the God who led them out of slavery in Egypt, the God who provided for and protected their nation for years. They were not to trust in the technologies of war, treaties with Egypt, or chariots and horses and armies, but in God. Though we find ourselves in different circumstances more than two thousand years later, God asks us to do the same. When we are faced with challenges that we cannot handle, situations that threaten to undo us, God wants us to take refuge in Jesus, who poured out his blood and gave his life to bring us into right relationship with his Father.

But so often my heart is unwilling. I would rather run the other direction, or dig in until I'm the last lonely person standing on a mountain I'm willing to die on, a solitary signal on a hill, rather than take my refuge in God. I have had to learn to see God as my refuge the hard way.

When I quit taking refuge in God, it happened gradually. As though God were a friend I was really close to a year ago—talking on the phone and texting daily, and seeing each other multiple times a week. Then some small circumstance changed, and one day I see on her social media page that she is engaged or about to have a baby, she has been working at a new job for a while, or she is up and moving to Africa, and I realize with shock that I haven't made contact in *forever*. I never meant to lose touch with God. I was just so frantic trying to keep up with daily life that I forgot to call. When I did remember, I was always in the middle of something else. It started to feel overwhelming to catch up on all I had missed. When I had to cancel a few of our dates last minute, it was just too hard to reschedule. My life looked totally different these days.

God probably wouldn't even understand. When I thought

about spending time together, I no longer felt excitement and joy, I felt guilt, sadness, and anger at myself.

A lost friendship seems like the best analogy because this shift in my relationship with God changed at the same time that a lot of my relationships changed: when my first child was born. Like many first-time parents, I found my life change and my social circle contract drastically. It was harder to make it out to activities that I enjoyed when I was single or childless: long coffee chats, nights out. It took me an hour to pack up baby and diaper bag and get out the front door, then I turned right back around again to tend to a dirty diaper or to give another feeding. Friends moved away. Clint got a good job as a youth pastor at a new church, but we found it hard to get to know other adults. Clint worked two other jobs as well. The baby wouldn't sleep at night. I healed from my painful C-section, but I got a recurring infection that required minor surgery. My life was changing so fast that I wondered who I was anymore. I couldn't count on work outside the home, a career, or an income level to form my identity. No one was offering any pats on the back or gold stars for a brilliant job scrubbing spit-up stains out of baby clothes. In fact, I was disappearing entirely under piles of laundry, diapers, meal plans, compost, and dishes. Left in the silence and stillness of my own heart, I realized that I didn't even like myself.

I felt abandoned by God. My hurt became hot and swollen. If I had picked up the phone, all I had left was pain and anger. So I didn't.

God just wanted to hear my everyday voice, no matter how angry, but I was too turned in on myself to see it. Immanuel was *always* there when I called. God my Friend was, in fact, just outside the door knocking if I'd only unlock it.

Trust is a relationship. In order to build trust, I open up, just a little, and show myself for who I really am. I share. My messy emotions. My strong feelings. My weakness. My wounds. God listens. Then God opens up to me a bit more, revealing more of who God really is. God's uncomfortable love. God's blinding glory. God's weaknesses and wounds. I listen. Relationship changes me.

This section of the book focuses on building trust relationships with God and with others, through attentive, quiet good deeds. God waits to be gracious to me and to you. The Sovereign Lord waits patiently for us to open the door, lift our flushed faces, and look love in the eyes.

Listen to someone you love

Check in with a spouse, a roommate, a family member, or a friend by asking about the highlight and lowlight of their day. In one way, this task seems too simple. If you have followed the course of the book, you have already written letters, given gifts, and spent time remembering with friends. But this is an important tool for those of us still learning to listen, to stretch toward one another with concern and to give our full attention. This question works well when your spouse or roommate has returned home after work, when you pick up a child from school, as you are cooking dinner, when the family sits down to dinner, or before you settle into watching TV and poking around on social media feeds.

In her book *How to Talk to Practically Anybody About Practically Anything*, Barbara Walters shares a truth that has stuck with me since I read it as a shy young woman: People love to talk about themselves, and especially to share their stories and experiences with someone who will listen carefully. Walters found this equally true whether she was meeting celebrities, making daily conversation, or interviewing people for TV. She was always looking for the next good questions that could get a person talking about themselves.

Walters's principle can help us build daily connections with people we love. If I ask, "So what was the highlight and the lowlight of your day?" and genuinely listen—without trying to fix problems, judge mistakes, or jump too quickly to my own stories—the people in my life love having a chance to talk about themselves. They love to commiserate about what frustrated them that day. They love to connect and share about the small victories of everyday life. It's a beautiful thing to feel like someone cares enough to ask about our day and to listen to what we have to say.

Listening requires a much more focused kind of attention than the other practices in this book. It can be draining for the sufferer of spiritual ADD, but important.

To listen to others and give them our close attention is the foundation of all trusting relationship. We listen to those we love: they listen to us in turn: trust is built. God listens to us, we listen to God: trust is built. And when the day comes that we need safe refuge, we can find it. In God and in our loved ones. Because we have not neglected healthy relationships.

My friend Shannon taught me the power of asking people about highlights and lowlights in a weekly small group Bible Study she led. Most weeks as we sat on the couches and floors in our friend Michael's apartment, Shannon would start off our time by asking: "What was the highlight and lowlight of your week?" Before we opened up God's Word together, we would slowly move around the room and share the best and the worst of our daily lives. It was a much more effective question than "How can we pray for you?" because it was more specific, easier to answer, and free of stuffy language about praises and prayer requests. Instead of trying to give the "right" answer, we just gave honest answers: We told about our struggles with unemployment, housing, food poisoning, family relationships, pregnancy aches and pains, infertility, work woes, singleness, surgeries, deaths, and grad school exams; we shared about life's small victories such as exciting research projects, passing grades, fun trips, job opportunities, baby showers, new relationships, healed wounds, races run, future hopes, and drama-free days at work. Each member of our group shared and listened in turn. And slowly, over the course of about two years, we built a strong bond of trust with one another.

These friends cheered on my creative writing, celebrated my graduation, and came to our home to celebrate the Anglican service of "Thanksgiving after Childbirth" with us when our daughter was born a few months later. They showed up for her baptism, gave her gracious gifts, and cuddled her like proud family members. And when I got sick unexpectedly, they were the ones we sent a panicked e-mail to, even though *technically* we weren't even a part of the group anymore. These were the people we trusted and the people we knew would help. They cleaned our house, explained our medical care options, found us a good family doctor, and checked in on us in the months that followed. Our honest practice of showing up, sharing, and listening to one another had built relationships of trust and care we could rely on when crisis came, and we weren't the only ones to call for help during those years. The group didn't last forever—the push and pull of school, careers, and housing changed the group over the years—but I'm grateful I could experience the Body of Christ in that way in the years I needed it most. The friendship build by our honest conversation became a refuge when tough times hit.

Make space for the question "What was the highlight and

lowlight of your day?" Ask follow-up questions that show you were giving your full attention to what your loved one says, simple things like: "Huh. What did you think about that?" "Hmm…What did you mean by this?" "Wow! How did that make you feel?" "Oh no! What are you going to do?"

Close the computer and put your phone out of sight. Silence your notifications for ten minutes or so, no interruptions. Give your *whole* attention. Put away thoughts of being anywhere else with anyone else. These thoughts are an insult to the person in front of you, who is eager for you to really hear them, respond to them, and love them. So set aside your tech for this ten minutes. Be present *here*, not anywhere else.

As you listen, keep in mind that what people hope for when they tell their stories is what we all hope for, to know that whatever is going on, they can count on us to be with them. In their joys and in their pains, laughing and crying. We are listening.

Listen for the monastic bell

It is tempting to imagine that in the ideal spiritual life, hidden away from the world in a monastery, monks and nuns experience absolute peace and freedom to choose what they do with their time, freedom to pray all day long or to *just be* with God. Often we think this way because this is what we long for ourselves. But a monk does not choose how to spend all the hours of his life. While he makes big promises to love God and to give his life to serve, monks are still only human, with bodies, friends, homes, and communities to tend to.

In a monastery the monk's life is often ruled by the call of a bell, a little like a student's or a teacher's life is ruled by a bell. As Ronald Rolheiser describes, "Whenever the monastic bell rang, [the monks] were to drop whatever they were doing and go immediately to the particular activity (prayer, meals, work, study, sleep) to which the bell was summoning them. . . . If they were writing a letter they were to stop in mid-sentence when the bell rang. . . . When the bell called, it called you to the next task and you were to respond immediately, not because you want to, but because it's time for that task and your time isn't your time, it's God's time."* This bell does not just sound for monks, but for all of us. As Rolheiser has written elsewhere, it teaches us the same lesson: "To stretch the heart by always taking you beyond your own agenda to God's agenda."†

Submit your agenda for your day to the bell that calls you to one more daily, repetitive good deed.

To listen for God's bell is to listen to the rhythms of your everyday life—the cry of a child, the ring of the phone, the tone of the alarm clock, the rhythm of leaving for work, car-pool lanes and transit rides, daily errands, meals, chores—as though they were a bell. When the bell calls you to the next thing, you drop what you are doing, and move on. This is harder than it seems at first glance.

I often resent the bell. It rings in my ears like a nag. "Hurry up, hurry up, there is never enough time." "Keep up, keep up, you are getting behind." When the bell rings, it reminds me I am not in control. But I *like* to feel like I'm in control. I would rather hit the snooze button on the alarm clock and tell it, "You don't control me, I'll get up when I'm good and ready." I would rather tell my loved one, "Calm down, I'll get to you when I get to you." I would rather do what I *want* to do, and not what I *have* to do. I resent things that simply have to be done.

Like making my daughter's lunch. Every night before I go to bed, I need to make sure that either my husband or I have made my daughter's lunch for the next day. It is a simple enough task, because she has basically the same things in it every day: a small nut-free sandwich, a baggie of chips, a yogurt or cheese, a fruit or veggie. But making my daughter's lunch irritates me. It pulls me away from what I enjoy doing in the few quiet hours between the kids' bedtime and my own. It's the time of day that I like to think of as "my time," the time I like to control. Plus, I almost always forget about the lunch. Then my husband has to gently remind me and I catch myself grumbling at the stupid bell. I was enjoying myself there, doing whatever I wanted. It's annoying to be interrupted.

In that moment, I feel a loss of control like I felt often in my first year of teaching. Inner-city teaching was no picnic for a young woman like me who was educated in mostly Christian schools in comfortable suburbs. As a new teacher, I worked long hours planning lessons from scratch; I fielded demands from students, teachers, principals, and parents; and I pulled all-nighters to keep up with grading. The ring of the bell signaling the next class period often took me by complete surprise. I never felt I could finish anything before the next thing called, and I headed toward it with bitter resignation, one foot in front of the other. That year, I spent a lot of time in subway stations on the way to work wishing that I could be that businesswoman with her briefcase or the child on the way to school. It felt like I would have to become an entirely different person to be happy, to have freedom and control over my own life again.

What listening for the monastic bell calls me to remember is that my life is not my own. My time is not my own. Even my to-do list is not my own (as good as it is to have one). My life belongs to God, it is worth a lot to God, and God calls me to the next good thing. And these *are* good things. Good in my life as a teacher and good in my life now. Punching my time card, making parent phone calls, following up discipline issues, feeding my body, planning tomorrow's class, grading today's papers, and saying hi to my coworkers—all good.

Emptying dishwashers, changing diapers, making lunches, wiping out sinks, going to bed at a decent hour, waking up to work, answering e-mails, putting Band-Aids on boo-boos, listening to my husband, going to church—all good. All these things limit my freedom and my control over my own life. But all of them make my life and the lives of others better in a real and tangible way.

Listen for the ring of God's bell as it calls you to embrace the life he has given. Not the life you wish you had if you were in control, but the tough, beautiful life right in front of you.

————

*Ronald Rolheiser, *Forgotten Among the Lilies: Learning to Love Beyond Our Fears* (New York: Crown, 2007), 116.

†Ronald Rolheiser, "The Domestic Monastery," January 7, 2001. http://www.lifeissues.net/writers/ron/ron_14domesticmonastery.html.

Imagine you are with Jesus in a Bible story

See, hear, taste, touch, and smell life with God through a story from Jesus's life. We can do this thanks to the eyewitnesses who set down their fishing nets, paid out their tax businesses, and gave up their own lives in order to follow Jesus around every day for three years, to watch his life carefully, and to learn from him. Lucky for us, these men wrote down the strange and unbelievable things they saw.

Our imaginations are an important resource for interpreting the vivid stories these eyewitnesses have passed down to us. Because imagination requires and builds our discernment. Discernment is like a muscle—we need to use it regularly for it to grow stronger. If we only rely on others to tell us what to believe or how to recognize God in the world, our discernment muscle will be weak. If we do not spend regular time with Jesus, we will not know how to recognize him in the crowd in a time of urgent need. We will not be able to take refuge in him. So put your imagination to good use!

As you face this task, you can choose any story from Jesus's life, but I've included below an example from Luke 13:10–17. Find a comfortable place to sit. Hold the Scripture passage in your lap and close your eyes to focus. You could also try a recording, but make sure you can pause it to reflect. You don't want to rush this.

When you are comfortable and ready to start, take a few deep Spirit-breaths. Thank God for being present with you today. Ask Jesus, "Can I just hang out with you for a few minutes?" Pause to hear his response. Ask God, "Could your Spirit help this story come alive to me in my imagination?"

Let your eyes fall down onto the passage in your lap, or hit Play on a recording. Read the words of the passage aloud several times. Let them soak into you like water into the soil around the roots of a plant.

> [Jesus] was teaching in one of the meeting places on the Sabbath. There was a woman present, so twisted and bent over with arthritis that she couldn't even look up. She had been afflicted with this for eighteen years. When Jesus saw her, he called her over. "Woman, you're free!" He laid hands on her and suddenly she was standing straight and tall, giving glory to God.
>
> The meeting-place president, furious because Jesus had healed on the Sabbath, said to the congregation, "Six days have been defined as work days. Come on one of the six if you want to be healed, but not on the seventh, the Sabbath."
>
> But Jesus shot back, "You frauds! Each Sabbath every one of you regularly unties your cow or donkey from its stall, leads it out for water, and thinks nothing of it. So why isn't it all right for me to untie this

daughter of Abraham and lead her from the stall where Satan has had her tied these eighteen years?"

When he put it that way, his critics were left looking quite silly and red-faced. The congregation was delighted and cheered him on. (Luke 13:10–17 MSG)

Once you have read the passage several times, daydream your way through the story in the passage. Stop to ask questions as you move line by line through the story, and pause to listen for God's Spirit to answer. I've included my questions here, to give you the idea, but ask your own too.

Here is what imagining this passage may look like:

- Picture the scene in your mind, as though you are there. Keep your eyes on Jesus.
- Where is he? Can you spot him over there?
- What is **the meeting place** like?
- Can you see her, on the other side of the room, the woman who is **twisted and bent over**? What do you notice about her?
- Jesus is calling her. "**Woman, you're free**!" What could he mean by that? Why *those* words?
- Look! **He's** *touching* **her**! And—what in the world?! She's **standing straight now, tall**, her head held high! How does the room feel different? Can you hear the others? What are they saying?
- Uh-oh, **the leader of the meeting place** sure doesn't look happy. Why is he so **furious**? What does **the Sabbath** rest seem to mean to him?

- Whoa, Jesus is angry, too! What is he saying? What's this about **the cow and donkey**? Has this woman been **tied up**? What does **Sabbath** rest mean to Jesus?
- Look at the leader. How is he changed? Look at the crowd. How are they changed?
- Look at the woman again. How is she changed?
- Look back to Jesus. Is your heart changed?

As you finish, it may feel a little bit like you dove down deep into a swimming pool and you are coming up to the surface again. Take a moment to thank Jesus that you could spend time with him. Ask him if there is anything else. Ask yourself, what you have seen or understood through this time with Jesus that you couldn't see before?

End with a grateful "Amen!"

This task is powerful whether you are alone, with a partner, or in a group. In a group, one person can lead with questions, while the rest sit silently, eyes closed, and listen. Stick to the story. At the end you can share your impressions with one another. Imagining together with others provides an added layer of accountability, to keep your mind from wandering and to keep yourself from wandering off into theological hot waters.

So how do we know if something is the "right" way of thinking about a passage? Study can help, but the best kind of study is not a scientific examination of each word and its absolute meaning; it is an imaginative encounter with Jesus himself, the person of the Gospel, the Word of God, which allows us to put ourselves in the shoes of the original witnesses of Scripture.

Write down a dream, a feeling, or a worry that weighs on your soul

Spend some time writing down what weighs heavily on your soul.

It could mean jotting down a dream you had this morning, just as you were waking up, that you just can't figure out. But what you saw felt important, as though God was trying to get a message through to your subconscious. You can't ignore it.

Or maybe your soul feels tied up in knots, heavy with emotions, thoughts, and ideas. Difficult news stories have given you that helpless feeling that lives are at stake and you can't do anything about it. Maybe you are personally going through something painful, a loss, a grief, a devastating heartbreak. Maybe you are just confused about how to make a decision, or how to survive the anxious tension that you feel, or how to make it through the day when you just want to head back to bed and have a do-over.

Maybe you know that you are repeating to yourself things that aren't true: "I'm all alone, no one loves me," "This is too hard, I can't do this," or "I'm too stupid/emotional/unstable/weak/small." But you can't figure out how to quiet those negative thoughts and find peace in your soul.

In all these situations, and many more, find a blank page and a simple pen, and write down, honestly, with no filters and no shame, what you are thinking and feeling. Give your-self your full attention. Start right here, where you are. With your anger (at God, yourself, others), your sadness, your frustration, your weakness, your shame, your grief. Let those things out, onto the page. Don't worry about proper spelling or punctuation or whether anyone is ever going to read these things. Don't let your internal editor tell you, "Don't write that down, that sounds stupid." Put in your imaginary ear plugs and just write.

Face yourself how you really are. Take off your masks. Write through to the big questions: "Who?" and "What?"; "When?" and "Where?"; "Why?" and "How?" How *did* you get here? Why does this feel like it does? Try to identify what is needed—not to *fix* yourself or your problems or your strug-gles, but to live beyond them, to refuse to be eliminated by them, to reject the voices that are trying to bring you down.

Trust yourself enough to say what needs to be said. Then, when you have found a little bit of quiet, turn your face to the One who created you. Read what you just wrote out loud. Unleash on God your angry words, your hurt, your pain, your sadness. Turn to God honestly, just as you are. No pinching, brightly polished Sunday shoes or neatly starched and stiffly ironed Sunday dress, no clean, tight, itchy Sunday tie. We are trying to unlearn the lessons we learned as squirming kids in church when we were told to come as we were not, when we thought we were only welcome in the world of mature relationship with God when we had it all together.

Taking refuge in God requires and presupposes that we do *not* have it all together. In fact, it implies that things are falling apart. We take refuge when the enemy army is upon us, when our neat plans for our lives fall apart, when, as the poet W. B. Yeats put it, "the center cannot hold." At those moments we are faced with a choice. We can stay and suffer alone, we can gang up with others to make a rational new plan to fix things, or we can run to God.

There is a stubborn part of me that would rather run just about anywhere else. Just please *not* God. Jesus knows way too much about me, way more than I ever wanted him to see. He won't leave me alone. I could be happy without him, I'm sure of it. And if I'm not, well then, I'd rather suffer alone, with my dignity intact. Why can't he *leave me alone*?

But when I'm honest with myself, those thoughts are absurd. There is nothing I long for more than God's love, even if I wish it didn't hurt so much. God's love hurts because it requires me to acknowledge that like a young child who can't survive without adults in her life to feed, protect, teach, and care for her, I can't make it without God. Those are the terms. They are not fair. I sure would like to think that I'm more than a helpless child. I want to believe that I'm stronger than that. That given long enough, I could make it on my own.

But I can't. I gave it my best shot and here I am. Weary. Exhausted. Angry. Overwhelmed.

So I write to take refuge in God. On a Friday afternoon on my train ride home after a grueling week teaching school, when I can feel the weight of responsibility lifting off me at last. At the end of any long day, when I would so much rather bury everything under a wave of distractions—movies, TV series, social media, news articles—instead of opening up the windows of my soul so I can breathe fresh air as I go to sleep. I write to take refuge in God when I need to figure out a problem or an emotion that is hijacking my life. After an argument or conflict, after a long day, after reading something online that got me going. When there is something I specifically want to write through, or when I want to discover what it is that sent me to the page in the first place.

Only you know what you may need to write down, what you are thinking or feeling, or which part of your soul needs to be listened to. But writing can be holy work. Not only for professionals, but for every average soul who struggles to take refuge in God.

Give up what you can't imagine living without

Make a plan to give up an addiction, a bad habit, or a guilty pleasure that is a part of your daily life, but isn't ultimately good for you.

When I took stock of my life four years ago, I immediately knew something needed to change. And I knew what needed to change. I definitely did not want it to change.

After putting our daughter to sleep one night, Clint came into our tiny bedroom looking for me. He found me lying on the bed, stiff as a board, fully clothed, but hiding under our duvet, which I had pulled up to my chin. My eyes were huge and round with genuine fear.

"Umm...What are you doing?" Clint said, stopping to look at me in confusion (and trying not to laugh).

"I think God wants me to give up Facebook," I said quickly. I added with a melodramatic sigh, "But I don't *waaant* to give up Facebook! And besides, I don't even know if I can. How in the world would I be able to keep in contact with all my friends and even my family? Won't they miss me?"

While I lay there, I was having this little fight with God. I am one of those people who find social media (and sometimes the whole Internet) hopelessly addicting. I don't think I'm alone, but I haven't met very many people who admit it openly. When I log in to my Facebook account, I spend more time than I think is healthy. Every. Time. A little bit of this is because I have high standards for how I spend my time, and I feel guilty when I feel I've wasted time. But the true story is that, left to myself, I spend *hours* online. Time, like any other limited resource, needs to be budgeted. I want the freedom to say, "That is not how I choose to spend my time." I want the freedom to answer when God calls me to the next good thing. And that night I knew I didn't have those freedoms.

The quality of my life was suffering. My face-to-face relationships were hurting. Instead of calling for a chat, writing a note, or planning a get-together with a friend, I was spending my time on my Facebook newsfeed, which never seemed to run out. I don't want to diminish the fact that this was a way of connecting with people. I sent many personal messages. I chatted with friends far and near. I was grateful to see the shared articles and opinions and even rants, to hear from my friends what they were thinking or what they were up to these days. But when I finally closed my computer at the end of each session, I came away feeling distracted, overwhelmed, unable to focus, upset by comments I had seen or news I had learned. I knew that I was turning to Facebook whenever I felt bored, when I should have turned to conversation with my husband, playtime with my daughters, quiet time alone, or the good work I needed to do in my home. Those valuable experiences just couldn't compare with the excitement of liking, sharing, and "connecting."

My soul could not handle it anymore.

But I also felt afraid that, without Facebook, I would be alone.

This wasn't true, but it felt like it was true. I was scared to death, lying there on my bed. Giving this one small thing up, this thing that was coming between me and God and healthy relationships with others, felt like a very painful mini-death.

Technically, giving up Facebook was easy: done in ten minutes. I sent out a few messages to my friends, then Clint downloaded my account information onto a flash drive, changed the password for my account, and deactivated my account. There were some hiccups. Messages and posts disappear after an account is deactivated, so my friends couldn't access a link to my blog, where I had written about why I was leaving. I found myself in approval withdrawal. How was I going to know if what I was doing every day was valuable if I couldn't post it online and get likes for it? Where was I going to record this brilliant thought I had today if not in a status? How would I know I was still real if I didn't have an online presence?

These questions sound silly in hindsight, but they were important to me then. Sometimes souls stretched to their limits throw tantrums like little children. Don't take it out on other people, but don't be afraid to be honest with yourself either. If God is not your refuge, if something else has become the place you run when you are in trouble—then that thing is an Idol, an addiction, a problem. It needs to go, at least for a while. Until your soul can calm down and get some perspective.

I am back on Facebook again these days, but I still ask these questions from time to time. When I started using social media again, I was glad that I could see differently than I had before. I found it easier to manage. For a little while. Then I had to figure out how to make some new boundaries. For the most part, that is working.

In *Confessions*, Augustine famously said, "Lord, make me chaste...but not yet." He knew what wasn't good for him anymore, but felt he wasn't quite ready to give it up. My prayer might be, "Lord, help me get off Facebook permanently... but not yet." Or, "Lord, help me to quit eating foods that hurt me...but not yet."

Each of these things is controversial, personal, unique. Not everyone has to give up sex, or the Internet, or sugar, or alcohol, or whatever else. But for each of us, there is at least one normally good thing that we *do* need to give up. And if we can invest ten minutes identifying what that is and giving it to God, then that is a start.

What do you run to for refuge instead of God? Give up what is hurting you, and take refuge in God instead. Start small and see that God is present to us in the weakest places of our souls.

"So . . . What Happens Next?"

Abraham has a conversation with God in Genesis 12 that shows the power of a trusting relationship. When God called them, Abraham and Sarah left their home, traveled hundreds of miles on foot or by camel, and they were waiting for God to make good on promises: a home, a son, a family. But God does not seem to be in any hurry at all. They are growing weary.

Then God meets Abraham one night and reaffirms the promise: "Don't be afraid, Abram, I am your shield. Your reward shall be very great." God listens to Abraham, who doesn't see a way forward. And God makes the impossible promise again: "Look toward heaven and count the stars, if you can. That's how many descendants I have in mind for you." Then the story says, "And Abram believed the LORD and the LORD credited it to him as righteousness."

Righteousness is the kind of word I squint at and think, "Isn't there some other way to say it?" The simplest way of thinking about it is that righteousness just means "right-relatedness."

Abraham might have thought God was crazy, that what God was saying was absolutely nuts, impossible.

But hey, God is *God*.

So far on their wild journey, God had never left them. It even seemed like God loved them, which was decidedly not because they had accomplished awesome feats in God's name. They had made a mess of things more than once already. Yet here was God again, showing up to say, "Do not be afraid." God could take away the dark, swirling fog of their doubt and trouble with one breath, with one simple thought, but it didn't seem like that was the plan. God seemed perfectly okay with the fog, as if the All-Powerful One would rather save the energy and do something completely beyond what Abraham could imagine.

"Okay, fine, God," I imagine Abraham might have said, feeling trust burn like something tiny, bright, and hot inside his chest. "So...what happens next?"

Turning our hot, red, angry faces back to God is not glamorous. It hurt to admit that I locked the door that kept God out of my life when I was deeply in pain and that I sat down slumped against it. God's healing took me places that I did not want to go. God asked of me things I did not want to give. Opening myself up to God's love hurt.

But while trusting in God requires a kind of death, without the willingness to look over at God and ask, "So...what happens next?" there can be no release from the hot, sticky tar of our own sin, guilt, and self-hatred. If we refuse to take refuge in God, we will never be able to experience the grace of life with gratitude. Without choosing right relationship and laying down our lives in trust, there can be no resurrection.

Rock a child to sleep

Sleep is one of the ultimate acts of trust. When you head toward sleep at the end of the day, the part of life that you can control, manage, and craft is over. As you sleep, you lie unconscious, inactive, and vulnerable. To let go and relax into sleep can feel impossible.

I never realized how much I struggle with sleep myself every night, until I had to teach two little people to sleep. The quiet moments just before my daughters' bedtime are both the best and the worst moments of my day. As I attend to their needs and teach them to fall asleep in trust, it dawns on me that I have sleep problems of my own I never noticed, problems with trusting God and letting go at the end of every day.

Bedtime moments with my daughters can be the best moments of my day because the quiet of bedtime creates a space for intimacy and attention in everyday ritual. On good days we dance and laugh our way through the routine. Splashing in the bath until fingers wrinkle up, brushing teeth, cheering for first attempts at using the potty. There are pajama songs, tickles and hugs, books and prayers, whispered secrets, and deep questions. Then, when the lights are out and the bedroom door is closed, Clint takes one daughter, I take the other, and we rock.

Rocking my children to sleep is one of the highlights of

my life. Once the lights are out and the songs are sung, my children lay their heads on my chest or my shoulder and relax into my arms with trust. I sing or hum and they gently drop off into sleep, secure in my love, sure that I will watch over them while they get the rest they need.

That's how things are supposed to go, at least. The quiet trust of bedtime is not as easy to achieve as we hope. There are plenty of nights when we shriek, boss, and cry our way through bedtime routine. I'm cranky because the bathtub splashes got me all wet, and now I'm cold. I'm tired from a long day. And I'm ready for these kids to get to bed so I can get on with all the things that I didn't get to today. But there are creepy shadows on the wall and wiggles that didn't get out yet, tosses and turns and stalling questions, and I feel like I could lose it.

But these moments when I am most tempted to bail, to turn my attention away to something more pleasant, these are the moments when reconnecting with my kids can build their trust. I rock them to get my energy out and pray with all my desperate soul that my little insomniacs will settle off to sleep. Eventually, even the toughest little one will drop off. Her head falls still and warm on my chest. Trusting. At peace. And I lay her in her bed with a prayer stuck like an ache of tears in my throat—"God be with her. Keep her safe."

Rocking my daughters to sleep in the quiet and the dark has taught me my own need to lay my head on God at night. Sleep for children *and* adults requires both attention and trust. We can't fall asleep when we're worked up, angry, distracted, or afraid. We have to feel safe in the dark and the quiet of night, as though things will be okay in the morning. As we sleep, we face our limits, and we are haunted by our ultimate limit: death. As a child, I used to shiver as I prayed the famous prayer "If I should die before I wake, I pray, dear Lord, my soul you'll take." But we prayed about death for good reason at bedtime. We have no guarantee we will be safe through the night and wake up in the morning. We can all use a little rocking off to sleep.

One traditional Christian prayer used at nighttime (and folded in near the end of the Anglican Compline service) is an odd little group of verses from Luke 2 called the Song of Simeon:

> *Now, Lord, you let your servant go in peace;*
> *Your word has been fulfilled.*
> *My own eyes have seen the salvation*
> *Which you have prepared in the sight of every people;*
> *A light to reveal you to the nations*
> *And the glory of your people Israel.**

The old man Simeon said these words after meeting Mary, Joseph, and the baby Jesus at the Jewish temple in Jerusalem. Like Abraham before him, Simeon waited a long time for God to fulfill a promise to him. God had promised Simeon that he would see the Chosen One. So Simeon waited at the temple with eager expectation and met every child who came there to be dedicated to God. For years. He was getting old. I'm sure he wondered more than once if God was still planning to keep the promise made not only to Simeon, but to the whole nation of Israel. Then one day, Simeon looked into the face of God at the entrance to the Temple, held Jesus's tiny body in his arms, heard his name—a common version of *Yeshua*, "God saves"—and spoke these words. "Now I can finally die at peace," Simeon said to God. "I know that you are a God who keeps your promises."

This is exactly what we need to remember every night as we head to sleep. God keeps promises. God kept the promises to Abraham, to Elijah, and to Simeon. Love got us through another weary day. We can lie down and sleep in peace.

Rock a child to sleep if you can, and as you rock, pray Simeon's prayer. Still your tossing and turning heart; lay your weary head on something soft: God keeps promises.

———

*Luke 2:29–32. The Archbishops' Council of the Church of England, *Common Worship: Services and Prayers for the Church of England* (2002–2004). Accessed via the Daily Prayer app for Android. Developed by Aimer.

Ask someone for help

What is it about us that makes it *so extremely hard* to ask for help?

I should be able to do life by myself. I was raised to believe that my life is not anybody else's responsibility but my own. I should be able to handle anything that comes my way. Up to a certain point in my life, that was true. Then *that* year hit. The one that was *too much*.

Suddenly, I reached the end of my abilities. We didn't have family nearby. We had just started at a new church. Beyond our old small group, I didn't know who to ask for help, so I tried to stick it out. "If I don't do this, nobody will," I mumbled under my breath with resentment while I washed the piled up dishes, clothes, and cloth diapers, while I scrubbed out the filthy kitchen sink or scum ring around the tub, and while I made yet another allergy-friendly meal from scratch. "If I don't do this, nobody will," I groaned as I stayed up all night with the baby *again*. "If I don't do this, nobody will," I complained to my husband as I did tasks that he had agreed to do but couldn't find the time for.

In a way, I was right. It was my responsibility to care for our home. I knew there were ways I needed to grow up and do the work. But I was also getting sick. I was completely exhausted and at my limits. I needed help. But I refused to admit that to myself.

Instead, I locked the door to my heart from the inside, one deadbolt at a time.

I didn't ask my hardworking husband for help, I lashed out at him in anger. Click.

I didn't ask my friends at church for help, I did whatever I could to end my comments and prayer requests on a positive note. "Oh, this is so hard, but I'll make it." Click.

I didn't ask my mom to come for a visit, I complained to her, "You never taught me to keep house, you did everything for me when I was little, now what am I supposed to do?" Click.

Alone and sobbing behind that door, I felt disgusted with myself. I burned with shame, self-blame, and self-hatred at my failure to handle my own life. When had I become such a mess?

The only key that can open a door locked tight by the phrase "If I don't do this, nobody will" is "Could you please help me?" I couldn't live like that anymore. I decided to open up in trust and ask for help.

Asking for help became one way I could open up again to the people who loved me and cared about me. For those of us who find it hard to build and rebuild relationships, I am learning to start out with small vulnerabilities. You put yourself out there in small ways with trust. You take off your mask, open the door, and shed the armor that you are hiding behind. Not all at once, if you can help it, but a little bit at a time. Hopefully, the person you open up to will open up a bit about something small in return for your trust. Then you can offer a little more.

Think of a quiet good deed that you can ask a friend, family member, or fellow church-goer to help you with. Borrow an ingredient from the neighbor for dinner. Ask a girlfriend to keep you company on the phone while you clean your bathroom or finish a boring task. Have your mom give you a wake-up call to help you get out of bed on time. Bounce an idea off your pastor before making a decision. Ask an expert if you have the right idea about God. Hire a counselor to help you work out some issues in your life that are too big for you. If you'd need help paying a counselor's bill, ask your sister or brother for support. Ask a retired friend to do a little babysitting so you can get an important errand or appointment in. If potty training your child or house training your pet is completely freaking you out, call around and get some advice. The list of small things that people who love you would be glad to help you with is long, if you could just get up the courage to ask.

The worst thing that could happen is that the person you ask for help slams the door of their heart in your face. More likely, if they can't help, they will say with genuine sadness, "I'm so sorry, but I can't right now." The courage to ask anyway despite your fears doesn't come from somewhere deep inside yourself; it comes from remembering that none of us can handle life on our own. A wise friend of mine says that her mom used to tell her, "Nobody can read your mind. You have to let people know what you need from them." At the very beginning, God said that it's not good for humans to be alone and created for us a community (Genesis 2:18). The point of asking for help isn't just to get the help. It's to unlock the door of your heart and open yourself to others. There is a risk involved, but also a responsibility. Once the door is open, it's your turn to listen, notice, and give your attention. Maybe you'll discover something you didn't know—that your friend is actually hugely stressed out or that there is something he or she needs from you: help, a listening ear, an apology, support, or the friendship you haven't been able to offer while you've been all locked up in your own problems.

You are not alone. But you may never know if you don't open yourself up to ask for help.

Say a creed aloud

We say a creed every Sunday at my church, and it never ceases to amaze me. All those accountants, farmers, laborers, business owners, scientists, musicians, lawyers, and teachers stand up and say that they believe in things that they never saw with their own eyes or heard with their own ears. They believe in things they never smelled or tasted, things that their hands never touched. They affirm that belief as they say the words of the Apostles' Creed:

I believe in God, the Father Almighty, maker of heaven and earth.

I believe in Jesus Christ his only Son our Lord, who was conceived by the Holy Spirit, born of the Virgin Mary, suffered under Pontius Pilate, was crucified, dead and buried; He descended into hell; The third day he rose again from the dead: he ascended into heaven, and sits at the right hand of God the Father Almighty, From thence he shall come to judge the quick and the dead.

I believe in the Holy Spirit, the holy Catholic Church; the communion of saints, the forgiveness of sins, the resurrection of the body, and the life everlasting. Amen.

As I stand there among my church friends saying these words, I wonder: How in the world could we ever be so *sure*?

To say these things, *in public*? To stake our lives on them? To share them with people *outside church* curious about what we believe? So many statements in the creed are apparently illogical, impossible one-time events.

Like most of the other things in the Book of Common Prayer, these words, and the fact that we stand together and affirm them in church, startle me yet again with a faith that is beyond what I would come up with on my own, a faith that challenges me with perspectives that are outside my small world.

The creeds are words put together by Greek-speaking Christians close to two thousand years ago. These faithful Greek believers met together at several church councils to determine the true story of Jesus's life—which of all the letters and books written in the first few centuries after Christ's life all Christians should read and study, and how we can remain faithful to the message of those books. And the Greeks aren't the only ones who had to make tough decisions. The English prayer book was written to reform the culture of the English Church five hundred years ago and to translate worship into the language of the common people. The people of faith who made these decisions were not perfect—there were fistfights and beheadings, political intrigues and wars fought over these things—but I believe that the best of them were trying to do what they could to listen to God and to seek God's face. Christians used the creeds and the prayer book to hash out answers to the toughest theological questions that faced them and to pass down to us a faith that was true.

Even if their questions and concerns are not the issues

that keep us up at night worrying, we still say the creeds and still use the prayer book, even when we don't feel a personal connection to them. Our difference from the original writers of these words allows us to learn from the perspectives of people from another time and place, to see what it meant for *them* to believe in God, to learn from their true stories how *we* can know God, and to affirm what we have in common as we look to God in relationship.

By saying the creeds and prayers, we repeat the true stories of God to one another again and again. That is, after all, why we come to church.

This dawned on me one Sunday morning a little while after I had wandered away from the Baptist tradition where I grew up and into a church in the Anglican tradition. That particular Sunday I visited the church my brother and his wife attended, a Baptist church. In some ways the worship was familiar, but in other ways it challenged me. Proud and hurt by previous experiences, I thought I could see so many things that were wrong with their ways of worshipping.

As we sat in the soft stackable chairs in a dimly lit room with a spotlit stage—a far cry from the hardwood pews and quiet old words where I met with God those days—I asked myself that morning, why do we even bother? Why come together week after week with these people whom we love and we can't stand, people who heal us and hurt us and who make us crazy? What are we doing here? Why not just give up?

Then, for just a moment, I let my wary heart actually listen for God's answer to that question.

We come to church to tell one another the story. We come to enter into the story of God's heart from the perspectives of people completely different than us from thousands of years ago—people such as Abraham and Sarah, Moses and Joshua, Ruth and Naomi, David and Bathsheba, Elijah and Isaiah, Peter and John, Paul and his co-laborer for Christ, Priscilla. Big characters, small characters. Men and women. The oppressed and the powerful. All loved, noticed, and attended to by God. All struggling to understand with their minds and hearts what it means to stretch toward God, to receive grace and live ready to serve.

The stories from the history of the church are important, too. Stories told by people such as Augustine and Bernard of Clairvaux, Julian of Norwich and Teresa of Avila, Thomas Cranmer and G. K. Chesterton.

The story of God in the world surprises us when we hear it from so many varying perspectives. It is difficult for us to give our honest attention to people who are not like us. It is more work to stretch toward them or even to understand them across the limitations of language and culture. We do not feel the immediate connection we feel with our kindred spirits—those with our personality type, our cultural and economic background, or our local heritage. God looks different in other people's stories and that scares us. Or God looks the same and we didn't expect to have anything in common. Our differences challenge us. This is why we need church—on a local, global, and historical level. To be offended by grace.

Stand up and say a creed. The Apostle's Creed above is probably the most popular, but you could also look for the

Nicene Creed or the Athanasian Creed. Look bravely for the truths of the creed in a local church on a Sunday. Whether or not they say a creed together, look for the story. It may be hard to show up in church, but give it a try. Make a stretch toward Christ's body in the world. Listen to the stories of others and tell your own story. Be challenged and be amazed. Let the stories of the saints throughout history, strange and wonderful, stretch your soul toward God. Let the stories of God's heart startle you into the Family.

Ask God your hardest question

James Houston writes, "To pray is to ask God to transform our lives."* When I started writing this book, I had no idea that at its heart it was about prayer. *Prayer* felt like a word that had lost all meaning. But the way to God is not what I'd expected. Every quiet good deed that stretches our hearts toward God can be a new way to pray.

Prayer eventually brings me back in my mind's eye to the basement apartment where I struggled alone, afraid to ask for help, sure in my miserable pride that I was a failure, a disappointment, and a mark against the people of God. I need to ask God my hardest questions. I look around the place, both familiar and strange after the passage of years. The ceiling with low painted beams, my desk, piled with papers and books, my old computer. My favorite poster of a woman in a flamenco dress. At the very front of the apartment is our round kitchen table with two candlesticks in the center, near salt and pepper shakers. The one south-facing window in the apartment washes the natural wood of the table with afternoon light.

A knock at the apartment door startles me. I see Jesus through the glass panes of the door, waiting. Our eyes meet, and he smiles.

"Hi! Would you like a cup of coffee?" I ask as I unlock the door and invite him in.

"Sure!" he says.

I put some water in a kettle and we make a little small talk as we wait for the water to boil. I grind coffee beans and pour them into the bottom of a French press. But I can't hold it back any longer. Skipping over pleasantries and getting right to the point, I state, "Jesus, I don't understand what you see in me."

Jesus's brown hands rest in the light on the table.

I am restless and unsure.

He smiles at me, like he's been waiting for this one. But he pauses to turn my comment back to me, "How do you see yourself, Laura?"

I sit down and think back to that lowest point. Back to the year of loneliness, despair, and my soul's locked door. Motherhood had overwhelmed me like a wave, stripping me of everything I thought I knew about myself. I feel myself fighting the wave, gasping for air again. Tears sting my eyes.

"I feel like a failure. I made so many mistakes."

"Laura, why didn't you take refuge in me? Why did you lock the door?"

"I don't know, I don't know." I turn away, pour the water over the coffee grounds, stir them together slowly with a small spoon. "Why won't you leave me alone?"

His silence presses gently on my wounded spirit. I take a deep breath; a chill of anger goes down my spine.

"It was her birth," I begin, turning toward him, sitting back down in the chair. "My oldest daughter's. I thought I had a handle on life, I thought I could manage it and control it. I had a perfectly healthy pregnancy. I avoided caffeine and sugar, I ate the right foods, I sat on a stupid exercise ball every day. I did everything right. Then the doctor came into my dim blue cave in the hospital's admitting room and I had no control anymore. She gave me choices I didn't want to make. The labor almost split me open with pain. I knew you were there, holding me. The Giver of Life. The one true Mother who gave his life on the cross to bear us into life that will never end, as my patron saint, Julian of Norwich, says.

"But then..." My voice quivers, my hands still, my eyes on the floor, "then my little baby almost died. We all heard her heartbeat slow down on the monitor. We held our breaths as we waited for each faint beep. And I knew I would do anything to save her life."

I hide my face in my hands.

"They took me into the operating room, stretched my arms straight out from my body. I was apologetic and ashamed. 'I'm sorry, I'm so sorry,' I told them. I shook uncontrollably from the drugs, the nerves, the joy, and the sadness. They cut open my side and gave her the life my body had failed to give. She was alive, but I was so afraid. The shadow of death fell over me that dark morning and I was so afraid."

I look Jesus straight in the face, my heart inside me stinging and cold. "I knew you were there, but you let that happen to me. So I closed the door."

The storm and wind and fire of these words slowly die down. A silence settles around us. I almost get up to get the mugs, but Jesus puts his hand on my arm.

"You are right," Jesus says, his voice breaking. "I was

there." I look and I can see that there are tears on his face as he looks out the window.

"Why didn't you do anything?" It was the question I most needed an answer to, the one I was afraid to ask.

"*I did,*" he replies, looking me in the eyes.

I can hear my daughter's first cry again, remember the rush of ecstatic gratefulness. Then the sinking feeling of my whole numb body screaming to jump up, to see her, to smell her, to hold her, to feel her slippery skin caked with blood. But the doctor continues her slow work on my belly, stitching my body back together. It is an eternity before the nurses hand me my daughter, wrapped tight in warm green terry blankets, her milky eyes squinting against the harsh lights of the operating room. My shaking fingers stroke her pale face and she looks at me and she is calm and alert, breathing normally and gaining color.

Her birth did not go the way I wanted. My body was weak and sore. Silent tears made my pillow cold for weeks, months, years afterward. My hurt pride thought it must have been my own fault. Surely I had done something wrong. If I had only asked to go for a walk. If I had refused the drugs and interventions. If I had borne up under the pain.

But who gave my daughter breath? Who did her blood belong to? My own blood, whose was that? Was it mine that I should protest? The realization was terrible, but I had it all wrong. When I came closer to death than I had ever been before, I did not take refuge in God, the Giver of Life, but turned my face away, unable to let go of my anger, to acknowledge my dependence, or to look my pain full in the face.

I got up without a word, pressed down the plunger of the coffee press slowly, filled the mugs. I poured milk into the cream pitcher, set it on the table next to the sugar bowl, and got two spoons out of the drawer. I cut us each a piece of the coffee cake I had made the day before and laid our places.

"You still haven't answered my question, Jesus," I said as I sat down. "How could you love me when I wouldn't even look at you? When I locked the door and nursed my failed pride? When I became so knotted up in my own ugly thoughts, I couldn't find a way out?"

"You cannot earn my love," he said. "I give it as freely as I give you your next breath, as I gave my body and blood on the cross for your nourishment. You cannot lose my love by your mistakes, your choices, your actions, not even death can ever separate you from my love. No fear can drive it out. No failure can shut it down. No sticky tar of self-hatred is so thick that my blood shed in love cannot wash it away. And I will never force you to love me back."

"How do I know it's real? It sounds too good to be true. A bunch of positive-thinking hogwash."

"Can you believe that I share life with you? Can you believe that my Spirit is present in your life every day as you close doors and open windows, work and rest, create and clean, eat and drink, plant and harvest, lie down and stand up? Can you believe that you are furiously, startlingly, freely loved and the gift of that love is life itself? Let love grow. Let it send down roots in your life. Let it throw out leaves. Let it be the dirt. The sun. The rain. The wind. Be rooted and grounded in my love day by day as you see its evidence in your life."

I look at him and sigh. "The only comfort I've found through these difficult years has been in making peace with quiet good deeds. I found love as I opened a window in spring to let fresh air into our apartment. And when I set the table for our meals. When I cut into an onion and cried. When I made space for a friend. When I went for a walk. When I laughed with friends, family, my husband, or my baby. When I showed up at church on Sundays as we read the old prayers and told the good stories. In the sunrise and the sunset. In the candle flame over the dinner table. In changing poopy diapers and pukey crib sheets. In nighttime prayers and lullabies. For a while now, I've done these things and been astonished to find your grace hidden in plain sight, so beautiful it hurt."

"Laura, where you saw failure, doubt, fear, and drudgery, I saw you faithfully picking up one foot after the other and learning one day at a time how to live like I live and how to love like I love."

Turn *your* face toward Jesus. Ask him how he sees you, where he was when something went wrong, or the hardest question you can think to ask. Make space within an ordinary moment of an ordinary day to unleash your storm, fire, wind, darkness, pain, and silence to the Lover of your soul. Turn to the One who sees you as you are. Rest in the Christ who plays in ten thousand places. Quiet yourself to hear the resonant voice of sheer silence. Place your trust in our Strong Refuge. Come away transformed. Not because questioning

Jesus will change everything, but because you are learning to be honest. To stretch toward God in love. To see all of life as a gift given freely, held in an open hand. Held not to save the world, but to save our own souls.

———

*James Houston, *The Transforming Power of Prayer: Deepening Your Friendship with God* (Colorado Springs, CO: NavPress, 1996), 247.

Plant a seed of peace

Plant a seed of peace. When you find yourself in conflict in your ordinary life—at work, while you are answering e-mails, in the middle of a heated argument with your husband, your wife, your roommate, your sister, your brother, your mom—plant a seed of peaceful relationship. When you find yourself leaning toward anxiety or worry. When you are tempted to anger or frustration. When you are hurt by someone's wrong actions and you want them to make things right. When someone is unpleasant, negative, or rude. When someone hasn't done their part. Plant a seed of peace.

At the beginning of this book, I encouraged you to plant a seed, so you may know from experience what planting is like. When you needed a seed to plant before, where did you find it? Did you make it from scratch? No, you had to go and find a seed at the grocery store, in your pantry, or in something alive in your daily life. And the seed's life—whether it was long or short—was ultimately a gift of God. It was not something you could control yourself, though you could foster it.

Seeds of peace are the same. Especially when we are weary and overwhelmed, we cannot control them. We cannot manufacture them ourselves. But we have strengthened the muscle of our attention in small, everyday tasks. Every time we have turned our faces back toward God, every time we have received loving forgiveness, rest, and quiet, we have experienced the peace of right relationship with God. That peace was not something we earn or strive for or struggle toward, but something we tend like a seedling growing in a cup that with water, sunlight, and love can grow into a mature plant.

I once had a little basil plant that I somehow managed to keep alive in a pot on my windowsill. I heard basil plants like sunlight and warmth, so I did my best to give it what it needed. I trimmed its leaves a few at a time and added them to my dinner. But I didn't use the whole plant, and I left alone the little purple flowers on the tips of the plant's stems. After a while, the flowers dried up into tough little brown pods. I wasn't quite sure what they were, but I didn't bother them. Eventually the whole plant sort of dried up and I began to notice little black specks on my white windowsill. When I looked closer, I saw that they were the basil seeds. At the right time those pods had split open and begun to spill their seeds. When I realized what was going on, I turned the whole plant upside down and shook out as many seeds as I could into a plastic bag, hundreds and hundreds of them from this one small plant.

Peace is something we can collect. We gather the seeds of peace—the ability to make peace where there is conflict and tension—from the gift of peaceful relationship that God grows in our own lives. When the plant has grown to maturity, by the careful attention God pays to our souls, letting Jesus's face shine on us, nourishing us with the living water of Christ, basking in the light of love, then by a miracle of grace, we'll begin to notice seeds of peaceful relationship that we can share with others. The strength to live at peace with others doesn't come from our striving or self-discipline. It spills abundantly from life at peace with God.

As we learn to live in relationship with God and see how God attends to our souls, even in our storms and distractions, we can learn to live with others in that same right relationship. We can sow seeds of peace.

The next time you find yourself in a situation that may spill over into tension and conflict, sow your seed of peace by giving your full attention to the person and the situation. Use all your practice from attending in everyday life to stretch toward this person who you would naturally want to recoil from. Turn your face to him. Really look at her. Not to pass judgment but with quiet curiosity.

Have some empathetic responses ready. Your words don't have to be fancy, something as simple as "Oh no!" or "That is so hard," or "That was too bad." Listen to your soul as it stretches toward the other person. At its core, to attend is to love. All this stretching is really just learning to love. Let your soul speak in its unique way to this person you are learning to love, even if it is just a sound, like "Ooooooh."*

Plant the seed of peace in the soil of daily life with gentleness. Don't respond to the conflict with answers or fixes or solutions. Respond with questions. "Tell me what *you* think?" "How do *you* feel?" Listen to the answers. Forgive this person in your heart. Hold out to God any offense they may have committed against you. Apologize if necessary. Be open.

Once the seed of peace is planted, remember that the growth is a pure gift of grace. The rest is out of your control.

Give the person in front of you the freedom and space to grow at their own pace. Let God do the work with their heart, leave consequences and judgments to the only Just Judge, and let God work in your heart, too.

God works out justice in the world through *us* and through our everyday struggle to treat each other with honor and dignity as we reveal God's Image to one another. Justice begins as we plant seeds of peace and heed the everyday call to *attend*.

———

*I'm grateful to the *Love and Logic* teaching and parenting curriculum written and presented by Jim Fay, Charles Fay, and Foster W. Cline for these empathetic statements.

Bodies in the World

For most of us, there is only the unattended
Moment, the moment in and out of time,
The distraction fit, lost in a shaft of sunlight,
The wild thyme unseen, or the winter lightning
Or the waterfall, or music heard so deeply
That it is not heard at all, but you are the music
While the music lasts. These are only hints and guesses,
Hints followed by guesses; and the rest
Is prayer, observance, discipline, thought and action.
The hint half guessed, the gift half understood, is Incar-
nation.

—T. S. Eliot, "The Dry Salvages"

Though relationship with God at the beginning of this book seemed like an impossible climb up a steep cliff, Isaiah 30:15 teaches us that relationship with God is more like an invitation to sit down with God at a table. When we first arrive, hungry and preoccupied, the table is set with crisp white linens and golden candlesticks, a table heavy laden with food—roast meats, rich vegetables, fresh breads, elaborate desserts. We can see the food and others eating the food, we can smell the food, we can touch the food to ensure it is what it claims to be and not a cardboard substitute, but we will not know that the food is good until we experience it with *all* of our five senses—until we taste it. We can choose to believe that the food is good and we can eat, or we can turn away from the meal, leave the dinner party behind, and go hungry.

This generous meal is laid out for you on tables groaning under the weight of it all. Your host approaches you with a huge smile, seats you in a place of honor, and begins to wait on you himself, making sure you have everything you desire. It feels strange. This is not what you expected.

Lift the fork to your mouth with your trembling hand.

Taste and see if the Lord is good.

The table God invites us to is not a banquet table every day, however; it is a family table. There are also days for simple meals: cookies and milk at the end of a long day, grilled cheese and canned tomato soup for a quick snack on the go, or for a thoughtful, allergy-friendly meal—everyday meals that make your eyes well up with gratefulness and satisfaction. There are also days where the table is cleared to make space for art projects, reading, or chatting over a cup of hot tea. There is space at the table for anger and tears, for illness, weakness, and need. For conversation and for quiet. This table is a space at the center of our family life with God, and it beckons all of us to stop for a moment, to attend to God and to our own simple needs, and to watch love transform our lives.

Every day, take one more bite—try one more quiet good deed—because what we do with our bodies in the world matters. The physical actions we take matter, and it matters when we pause to notice where God is already present in our lives.

Our quiet good deeds change us. They become our habits, build our character, and they reveal what we love.

The underpinning reasons *why* we do these things matter, too. They are not good or evil in themselves. We can orient these actions toward God or away from God. We can easily wash dishes, make beds, create, serve, or connect with people to serve ourselves—our own interests and idols—or we can choose to let these practices turn our faces to God.

God became a human being, incarnate and embodied, because God loves us and loves our frail bodies in this risky world. God longs to eat with us, and to see us filled with life and satisfied. God wants Jesus's body broken for us to be our spiritual daily bread, giving us the sustenance we need to get through another day. How we respond to God's love is our own choice. Just as you repeat the care of your body—washing, feeding, moving, resting—do not neglect to stretch your soul as you go forward. The next time you find yourself weary, restless, bored, sick, or unsettled in your soul, wherever you are, whatever shape you are in, turn your face toward God. Stretch toward God and keep stretching until it's a habit that forms your soul with discipline and satisfaction.

As you learn to attend to God, may you find peace, may you discover and rediscover the goodness and love of God, and may your humble offerings of returning, rest, quietness, and trust become conduits for God to pour out grace into your life. May you experience the power of peaceful table fellowship with God.

Acknowledgments

I would like to offer a few notes of thanks:

To Clint, my first reader, who is so patient with me, who supports my writing without wavering, and who loves me well. *Thank you.*

To my little girls, L and J, whose joyful spirits are contagious. *Thank you.*

To my mom and dad, Noreen and Dave, and Clint's mom and dad, Margaret and Brian, who invited us to live with them so that we could make space in our lives for my writing. Your gifts of time, money, food, and babysitting have made this book possible. We have lacked no good thing and your sacrifices have already been a blessing to many. *Thank you.*

To Adrienne Ingrum and the team at FaithWords, who have taken a chance on me and done a wonderful job with this book. In both ways, you are a faithful picture of our gracious God. *Thank you.*

To Pam and Chris and to John and Lorna, who have been some of the best friends that Clint and I could have ever imagined. It's been an honor to do life with you all—*in person*—during the past two years. *Thank you.*

To John Mason, Jonathan Smith, and those who put together, presented at, and attended the Anglican Connection Conference a few years ago. This book was born out of the rich conversations at the Conference a few years ago and John's many years of ministry in my life. *Thank you.*

To St Paul's Episcopal Church, Altus, Oklahoma, who have welcomed us warmly, showered our children with love, rejoiced with me as a writer, and offered space for me to write and work, especially Mother Suzanne Mollison and the *Altar in the World* book study group: Philip, Iva Nell, Bobbie, Nancy, Bonnie, Al, and David. And John and Paula. And so many more. *Thank you.*

To the early readers of *Attend*—Kevin, Ginette, Emily, Cindy, Brandiann, Kurt, Rachel, and Hannah—whose comments have helped me see in my blind spots and have made this book much better. *Thank you.*

To the Eli Lilly Foundation, the Collegeville Institute, workshop leader Lauren F. Winner, and each of the participants who helped me regain a hope for my writing that I had lost along the way. And Peter—who traveled a little way on the road of life with me and let me borrow a few of his words. *Thank you.*

To my teachers at Regent College, Cedarville University, and Covenant Christian High School. It's amazing to see my dream of publishing a book become a reality, and I couldn't have done it without you all, especially: Becky Fields, Andy Goodwin, Julie Moore, Don Deardorff, Maxine Hancock, and Rikk Watts. I also want to thank Peg Wilfong and Dan Chapman, who gave me C's on some of my first college writing assignments. It was devastating, and the best thing anyone ever did for my proud, stubborn heart. *Thank you.*

And to the Creator God, who in Christ by the Holy Spirit makes face-to-face relationships possible. *Thank you.*